finding GOD *in the* GRAY

The Lonely Path of Pain

FRANK FRIEDMANN

ISBN: 978-1-954869-01-1

Unless otherwise noted, all Scripture is quoted in NASB.
Add other translations used: ESV, GNT, KJV, MSG, NET, NIV, NKJV, NLT

This book is dedicated to all who have been forced to walk in a world they were not designed to live in, to those who have pain as their constant companion. I offer this book to you in brutal honesty. I make no false promises of deliverance from that which oppresses you daily, but I do extend an invitation for you to journey with me to find a way through your pain. Thank you for having the courage to go on this journey and for clinging to some semblance of hope that your story is still being written, that your pain will not have the last word.

"But You, LORD, are a shield around me,
my glory, and the One who lifts my head."

—Psalm 3:3

- CONTENTS -

When a routine colonoscopy revealed stage 3B colorectal cancer, the news for my friend Kevin East was surreal. He was young, healthy, and living a vibrant life. It wasn't supposed to happen to him. He endured eight rounds of IV chemo, six weeks of oral chemo, twenty-eight treatments of radiation, and then surgery to remove the tumor and infected lymph nodes. Just when he thought the end of his treatment was in sight, he received the frustrating news that cancer cells were still found in his body. Four more rounds of nauseating IV chemo were needed to "scrub" his body of any potential remaining cancer cells.

Jon Jenz, another dear friend, suggested that he and Kevin go skiing to get his mind off the agonizing treatments that lay on the horizon. On the last day of their trip, Kevin walked out onto frozen Lake Dillon in Summit County, Colorado. Jon could tell he was a bit pensive, so he lagged back behind to take this picture.

As he walked on the frozen lake, Kevin thought about how the surrounding scenery painted an accurate picture of how he felt. The lake was desolate. No footsteps accompanied him on this journey. It was cold and gray. The sun, hidden by massive cloud formations, labored to break through and provide him with its comforting rays of light. With each step, he could hear the ice cracking beneath him.

He pondered if the foundation of ice below his feet would hold. He wondered if he would drown as he stepped forward into the unknown. Fear was strong. Doubt filled his mind. He was alone in this journey. Being alone on that lake mirrored the feeling of walking through cancer. Although his loving wife, thriving kids, and community of friends continued to pour out their generous love, he couldn't shake the feeling of being alone.

Few people understand what is extremely hard to describe. The physical discomfort and subsequent treatment of cancer can be explained. But the future, potentially leaving his kids fatherless and his wife alone, weighed heavily on him.

Alone on that frozen lake, God gently reminded him, "When you feel cold and alone, press into Me. Walk toward Me. Keep your eyes fixed on Me. Receive My warmth and beauty in the midst of your pain." Even in the cold, loneliness, and fear of the unknown, Kevin stopped to soak in the rays of sun and the beauty around him. He embraced by faith that God was with him, and would continue to be with him, even though the pain and suffering threatened to overwhelm him.

Kevin did not know I was writing this book on pain. He was simply led to send me the picture. My soul was struck by the image I saw on my phone. Through Kevin, the Holy Spirit sent me the picture I had been searching for to be on the cover of this book. It captures the hearts of so many people who are walking their own lonely path of pain in the hopes of finding God in the gray circumstances of their lives.

Thank you, Kevin, for sharing your picture with me and giving me permission to put it on the cover. My hope is that the depths of the dark journey it depicts will call out to others on that same journey, that they will find God in the gray of their lives through this book. It is a joy to call you friend and journey honestly with you through life, with jointly held faith in our God, even amid the darkness this world can bring upon our lives. Bless you, Kevin.

- ACKNOWLEDGMENTS -

I extend a personal thanks to all those people over the years who have trusted me and shared their journey through pain with me. Your honesty taught me so much in learning how to compassionately embrace hurting people and speak the truth to them in love. Your journeys pushed me further down my own journey into the presence and provision of God, which are sufficient in my life no matter what this fallen world throws at me. Bless you.

Thank you, Jenne Acevedo, for another great job in editing my work. You faithfully tore my writing apart so I could put it back together in a way that would more fully capture my heart in presenting this as a tool to help hurting people. I am indebted to you for your expertise, even though you made me work really, *really* hard on this project. You are the best! I think I am looking forward to working with you again on our next project! I *think*...

Thank you, Josh Gordon and your team at Lazarus Media Productions, for helping with the formatting and cover design. It is a joy to work with you to bring the good news of Jesus to others. Your expertise in design work presents the heart of what I seek to communicate in my writing.

Thank you, Janet, Les-Leigh, Benjamin, Morgan, and Avery, my bride and my children, for the manifold patience and love you have extended to me as we share life together. The woundedness I brought to our family sometimes hindered me from being the husband and dad I longed to be to you. Your steadfast love and honor that you give to me has been a huge part of my healing and walking in the midst of pains that refuse to go away. You are amazing, and I love you with all my heart.

Supremely, I offer thanksgiving and praise to the Holy Spirit for fulfilling His role in my life as the Comforter. You comforted me in all things, and expressed Your life in mine to comfort others with the comfort You gave me (2 Corinthians 1:4). Thank You for Your ministry of life, regenerating me with the very life of God in me (Titus 3:5). I praise You for opening my eyes to the gift of Your own resurrection power that brings that life to me, even amid all the death that comes to me every day (Ephesians 3:14–20; 2 Corinthians 4:9–16). Thank You for being my teacher (John 14:26), for guiding me into truth so I could refute all the lies I had come to believe (John 16:13–15), for giving me Your strength in my weakness (2 Corinthians 12:9), for showing me what God was really like (Romans 8:14-16), and for giving me the power to understand the love God has for me, which is beyond comprehension (Ephesians 3:16–20).

Are you hurting? This was written with you in mind. You'll be changed by Frank Friedmann's radical response to the devastating pains of life. In this no-nonsense book, you'll see how the grace of God sits down with you until you're ready to walk again.

—Dr. John Russin,
Our Resolute Hope board member and wounded warrior

My friend, Frank: I've not met another human being possessed of a greater heart than he possesses—and readily shares. In the following pages, Frank does what Jesus did: he comes to where we are, engages us, seeks to understand, and stays until we find our footing and are able to walk again. There is a great deal of life in this book. A great deal of wisdom. More than enough heart to breathe life back into ours.

—Preston Gillham,
Writer and guide, PrestonGillham.com

If you are someone who has been blindsided by the pain in your life as a result of devastation and losses, regardless of what they are, this book will not only speak to your heart in a powerful way, but it will help you look at pain differently.

Finding God in the Gray will put to rest all your doubts and questions about God's love for you when bad things happen. This book will help you see straight into the heart of God even in those gray areas, the places of unanswered questions and spiritual conflict within.

I have known Frank for many years. I know his story. I've watched his response to the tremendous pain he has endured in his life, and I have been inspired! Only someone who has walked in the "valley of the shadow of death" is qualified to write about it.

—Yolanda Cohen Stith,
Co-Founder and Executive Director of New Heart Living, Inc., author of *Valley Life: Finding God in The Midst of Pain*

Finding God in the Gray was birthed not only from intense biblical study but also from Frank Friedmann's intimate experience with deep personal pain. As a pastor, he has helped many others get through the pain they could not get over. His book gives genuine hope for anyone who has been or is in personal pain. I highly recommend it to you as a must-read!

—Mark Maulding,
Best-selling author of *God's Best-Kept Secret;* President of Grace Life International, A Christian Counseling Ministry

I wish we could share a warm meal and discuss the pages of *Finding God in the Gray* together. Instead, I invite you into a journey through its deeply honest and glorious pages, because I am confident you will benefit from the wisdom that increasingly unfolds within.

I was in a season of trials a few years ago and needed help. I reached out to my dear friend Frank Friedmann and his bride to discuss the pages of my life. They invited me into a deeply honest conversation that led to comfort, wisdom, and a fresh breath of freedom that I deeply desired. At the end of our meal, Frank said he had more to share with me and would write me a letter.

Time passed, and one day he called and said my letter turned into a book. So here you have it. *Finding God in the Gray* is for all of us.

Please know that pain is pain. And if you haven't had a season of sorrow, you will. On planet Earth, no one escapes the many trials of life. But take heart, there are treasures to unfold as you read Frank's tender and wise words. They have arrived at precisely the right time.

—Tracy Levinson,
Best-selling author of *Unashamed: Candid Conversations about Dating, Love, Nakedness, and Faith*

This is such a good book because it is so raw and honest about how hard pain and grief really are! But the book also cuts through cliché theologies and grapples with the problem of pain more thoroughly, biblically, clearly, and sensitively than anything I have ever read on the subject. It is a rare jewel and so needed in the larger body of Christ.

—Kevin Brandon,
Pastor of Discipling and Care Ministry, Grace Life Fellowship, Baton Rouge, Louisiana

Soul pain cries for Spirit truth.

In *Finding God in the Gray*, Frank Friedman walks the reader on the lonely path of pain in the way, the truth, and the life of Christ. Compassionate, honest, and graceful, this book needs to be in the hands of the suffering and those who walk the lonely path of pain alongside them.

—Steve Pettit,
Pastor, director of One in Christ

We don't live in a kind world. It is a world where pain, disappointment, failure, and hurt are guaranteed. And while coming to Jesus for salvation, forgiveness, and new life is wonderful, it does not protect us or take away all our hurt. We need a way to address the pain. And this incredible book does just that. Frank shows us how we need to discover that healing doesn't come from running from or ignoring our pain. Rather, the hope, freedom, and relief we seek come from walking, and sometimes sitting, with Jesus in our pain. I can personally testify to the power of what Frank has written, and in the countless people I have counseled.

—Ross Gilbert,
Pastor, New Life Fellowship, Kitchener, Ontario, Canada

A refreshingly honest and vulnerable look into the problem of deep pain. *Finding God in the Gray* is sure to become a go-to resource for those of us who refuse to sugarcoat the truth about our very real suffering as we seek answers. We long for someone to simply "sit down with us" in our grief and confused torment. This author courageously does just that.

While refusing to deny the reality of the ache within, Frank Friedmann compassionately keeps the pilot light of hope burning consistently throughout the pages of this sacred literary salve. Maybe we really can learn to walk again after our greatest shattering. Maybe our story really is still being written!

—Sherri Irwin Feeney,
Widow, survivor of suicide and its devastating consequences

- FOREWORD -

Where do I begin?

I was walking through this world as a successful businessman. I was a well-respected leader in the community and was privileged to have influence in my religious community as well. I had a beautiful bride, precious children, and many dear friends. I was content, and life was wonderful.

Out of nowhere, a massive storm rose up on the horizon. In an instant, my children were gone. I had never known such pain and wondered if I would survive without them. In its gluttonous rage that storm consumed my business and all my possessions. My bride and I were alone and destitute. We cried so many tears that our tear ducts ran dry. The anguished heaving of our breath, however, did not cease. Wave after wave of convulsive sorrow pummeled us into the dust of the ground.

Precious friends did as friends will do. They rushed to our aid and sat with us in silence. They spoke no words. In such a time, they knew there could be no words. They wept with me and grieved with me, and I was so thankful for them as I tried to wrap my mind around what had happened. The questions swirled in my head, but there were no answers. Only a gaping hole in my soul. And if souls can bleed, mine surely did.

My sweet wife was overwhelmed in her grief, and we soon lost the cherished connection we had shared for so many years. I could not feel what she was experiencing, nor could she embrace the agony that consumed my soul. As the pain caused the distance between us to magnify, we learned that the path of grief is a lonely one.

As my misery continued, my friends turned miserable. They grew impatient with me and turned against me. They determined that I had sinned and demanded that I accept the blame for the great losses my family had endured. Their pontification was wrong. I had not sinned, nor had I brought this devastation on my household. I had nowhere to turn. I had no one to console or defend me, and my soul bled out. I was living life as a dead man walking.

I cried out to God, but heaven was quiet. The silence was deafening, confusion was reigning, and the pain grew more demanding. In agony, I tore my clothes and sat down in the dust of what was once a very blessed life. I screamed at the top of my lungs that I would never know joy again!

"Where are you God, and why is this happening? Talk to me," I cried out, longer and louder until, finally, I heard God speak from a whirlwind that sprang upon the horizon. He did not bring deliverance from my pain. Nor did he answer my questions. He hurled seventy-seven questions back at me. Questions about the universe, the stratosphere, oceanography, astronomy, and meteorology, for which I had no answers. I can still hear those questions. They are burned into my brain.

> Who is this who darkens the divine plan
> By words without knowledge?
> Now tighten the belt on your waist like a man;
> And I shall ask you, and you will inform Me!
> Where were you when I laid the foundation of the earth?
> Tell Me, if you have understanding!
> Have you ever in your life commanded the morning,
> And made the dawn know its place?
> Have you entered into the springs of the sea,
> And walked in the depth of the ocean?
> Have the gates of death been revealed to you,
> And have you seen the gates of deep darkness?
> Have you understood the expanse of the earth?
> Tell Me, if you know all this.
> Where is the way to the dwelling of light?
> And darkness, where is its place?
> Where is the way that the light is divided,
> And the east wind scattered on the earth?

From whose womb has come the ice?

And the frost of heaven, who has given it birth?

Can you bring out a constellation in its season?

Do you know the ordinances of the heavens,

Or do you establish their rule over the earth?

Can you send flashes of lightning?

Do you give the horse his might?

Do you clothe his neck with a mane?

Is it by your understanding that the hawk soars,

Stretching his wings toward the south?

Will the faultfinder contend with the Almighty?

Will you condemn Me so that you may be justified?

Or do you have an arm like God,

And can you thunder with a voice like His?

(Job 38–40 selected verses)

Silenced by the manifestation of how little I really knew, I embraced that He was not asking me for answers. He was revealing that I had none, except for Him. He was not calling me to understand but to bow my knees before Him. I was stunned by the awe of His grandeur and overwhelmed at His greatness and goodness! Then I understood. It was not my place to work this all out. That was His place as God. Mine was to surrender my heart in worship and make the choice to trust Him, for He alone is worthy of trust. I am too small to trust myself, and He is too big to not be trusted.

When I finally spoke, all I could say was that I had heard of Him before. I knew He was there, but I never understood how "there" He really was. Now I know that He is God. I know He is completely and unequivocally good. I know He is all powerful and reigning over the affairs of this universe. Though I may not understand, He knows what He is doing—and what He is doing is in accordance with His righteous character.

With faith in Him, I was finally able to stand up in my pain and ultimately walk into life again. It was different and would remain so. Knowing Him, I was able to get *through* what I would never get *over*. I miss my children terribly, and the tears still flow from my eyes when the memories of them come to the forefront of my mind.

I went back to work and was able to restore much of what I had lost. My bride and I learned to dance again, and we even had more children. Though they could never replace the children we lost, they light up our lives and bring joy to our hearts. Although I said I would never know joy again, I was wrong. In my sorrow, I am content and at peace.

It was my privilege to write the foreword for this book. The author has taken great care to deal honestly with the issues of hurt, loss, and trauma. He does not sugar coat the reality of our pain but continues to remind the reader if they trust God, God will meet them in their pain. He heralds to the reader from his own personal experience, that God will be faithful to them. One of the author's favorite phrases is, "God promises to be all that He is, to all that we need, in the moment of faith."

If you have been knocked down by the pains of life, whether they be physical or emotional, big or small, it does not matter. Pain can knock you down and keep you down. But if you are serious about finding God so you can stand up and walk again, I heartily recommend this book. As you trust Him, He will write the rest of your story.

I know what it's like to suffer pain, but through faith in God, I found joy and peace again. You can too. If you would like to read my full story, it is recorded in the Bible under the title that bears my name in the Old Testament. Shalom.

—Job

- INTRODUCTION -

I t is dangerous to write about pain. One who dares to do so must write cautiously. If he or she writes errantly, they will heap more hurt on those who are already buried under a mountain of pain. With that warning, I wrote a letter to a friend who needed help. Her marriage was on the brink of failure, her heart was confused, and her need for clarity was desperate. The more I wrote, the more I continued writing. Eventually that letter became the foundation for this book.

As I sought to create a tool to help people walk through their painful circumstances, I was constantly reminded of my own hurtful circumstances in life. My sorrowful memories had stung me sufficiently over the years and did not need to be brought into the present to continue their onslaught against me. My bride of almost forty years said she had not seen me so agitated in years. When she asked what was wrong, I told her the writing of this book was crushing me.

"Well then," she said, "get it done!"

After gritting my teeth, pouring my heart out on each page, and crying many tears, I did what she had urged me to do. The book was done. I asked some friends for their thoughts on it. Before even beginning that discussion, my dear friend Jim Fowler asked me what I learned from writing it.

My abrupt answer surprised me. I told him I learned that I had not trusted God very well in my pain, but through this project I was committed to trusting Him better. I pray through reading this book, you too will trust Him with your hurts, maybe a lot more than you have been, and in doing so, find God faithful to empower you in your journey.

It was not easy writing this book, nor will it be easy to read. As you have encountered things you will never get *over*, I pray you will find the God Who will help you get *through* those things. I pray that you find His presence, sufficient to empower you to live again.

Some have asked why I have not shared all the intimate details of my personal story of trauma in these pages. While I could do so, and did share some in chapter eleven, those terrible events no longer define who I am, nor do they bring me shame any longer. My life is defined by my standing in the finished work of Jesus, Who has made me acceptable and right. Further, this book is not about my journey, but yours. The details of my journey might cause you to focus on my experiences. You could conclude that compared to my pain, yours is insignificant. Or you might conclude that my struggles are insignificant compared to yours, and I could never understand your pain. This we must avoid at all costs.

We must never minimize our wounds. Nor should we conclude that our grief is so great that we are beyond the realm of moving forward in it. Our pain is pain to us. Our hurts must be embraced so we can bring them to God. I will not risk drawing your attention away from God, for He is the One Who alone can provide for you in the sorrowful experiences of your life. He is the only One capable of sheltering you under His wings. He is the only One who truly understands you and what you have been through. He alone can provide for you in your journey because He offers you Himself. You must find Him—because He came to find you and restore you to Himself.

My friend Steve Pettit masterfully declares: "Jesus did not come for the express purpose of dying for your sins. He came to establish and secure a relationship with you, and dying for your sins was the only way He could get that relationship."

This is Jesus's stated desire for you and for me. He wants an intimate relationship with us. He wants to share in every part of our lives. For too long, I hindered this from being my experience. I sought to hide from my past, ignore the nagging wounds, and deal with the sorrows in my heart on my own, independent of God. I pray this book will deliver you from that hindrance, and that you will finally and fully trust Him. May you find Him as the friend that sticks closer than a brother, the God Who hears the cry of your heart and stands ready to be a shield around you. May you find Him as the One Who is able to lift your head that is bowed down in shame and sorrow so you can see the light of His love and care for you. May He empower you to stand triumphantly over that which knocked you down.

In this book, I offer you Jesus. Nothing more. Nothing less.

May you come to know Him, as you have never known Him before. May you find Him to be sufficient, and even abundant, to provide for you as you journey with and through your pain.

I am sincerely in Him,

Pastor Frank

- OVERWHELMING PAIN -

Pain is painful. Pain can be overwhelming. Pain can be so devastating that it can drive us to desperate measures, even to the point of wanting to take our own life. If you have had suicidal thoughts, I am glad you are reading this book. I hope it will be a source of comfort and strength and lead you away from those thoughts and into the joy of living again.

If you are having suicidal thoughts right now, and it feels like you cannot go on, please stop reading this book and call the National Suicide Prevention Lifeline at 1-800-273-8255 or text HOME to 741741. Both are free and available 24/7. Please, call a friend, pastor or counselor and give them a chance to love you. You are worthy of that chance.

When you are ready, I hope you will pick this book back up and allow me to journey with you through your pain. My hope is that you will find God in a way you never knew Him and find the strength to get through what you cannot get over.

Free, Confidential Resources

National Suicide Prevention Lifeline

https://suicidepreventionlifeline.org

1-800-273-TALK

Crisis Text Line https://www.crisistextline.org

Text HOME to 741741

Network 220 Discipleship Ministries https://network220.org

American Foundation for Suicide Prevention https://afsp.org

Veterans Crisis Line https://www.veteranscrisisline.net

Note: These resources are current as of 2021.

- CHAPTER 1 -

The Experience of Pain

Pain can put you in a state of desperation. It can rock your world, push your mind into frantic overload, and throw your guts in a blender at high speed. All who sojourn in this fallen world will experience this in varying degrees. Some of those hurts will heal, and some we will carry to our grave. Some we brought on ourselves through our poor choices, while others were brought to us by the poor choices of others. Some will be easier to endure. Some will be so traumatic and so overwhelming that no amount of family support, Bible verses, prayer, or medicine can lessen their paralyzing grip on our soul. We can easily begin to lose hope when the cloud of darkness overshadows every waking hour and turns our night into a torrent of restlessness.

This intense emotional struggle treats you like a prisoner. You want to run from it as fast as you can and as far as you can, but the pain runs with you. It stays with you wherever you go. Day in and day out, the loss is there. Ominously and perpetually present, the traumatic circumstances that invaded your life seem to make time stand still. Where we used to not have enough time to fulfill the demands of our busy days, now it seems there is only time.

The devastation seems to have hit the pause button on our life's journey. The trauma we have endured just sits on the screen of our lives. It is impossible to rewind or fast forward to escape from that which has devastated us. *Pain.* It is just there, and it beats us mercilessly. We live walled in, suffocating, locked in a room we don't want to be in, with no key to open the door.

This timeless drudgery magnifies pain's effect. We were told by some well-intentioned false prophets that time would heal our wounds, but that was a lie. Time heals nothing. There is no way to alter what has happened, and no amount of time will assist us in "getting over" it. We must find a way through what we cannot get over.

I am not offering you an escape from pain. No one can. As the Dread Pirate Roberts said in my favorite movie, "Life is pain, highness. Anyone who says differently is selling something" (*The Princess Bride*, 1987). As human beings, we were designed to live in the garden of Eden, a paradise free from the presence of evil and pain. Planet Earth is no longer Eden. The paradise created for us by God has become a jungle full of "lions, tigers, and bears! Oh my!" (*The Wizard of Oz*, 1939). In this frightening jungle, every one of us experiences loss and hurt that we were not designed for. When we encounter pain that will not go away, it can leave us in a state of hopelessness. Hopelessness can lead to despair, and despair can cripple us for the rest of our lives. Somewhere, somehow, we must find someone who can restore our hope that the dreaded state we find ourselves in, is not the end of our story. This is why Jesus came.

Why Jesus Came

I often ask people to provide the supreme reason God sent His Son to this earth. The dominant answer I receive is that He came to die for our sins. That is a good answer. But I am not sure it is the best answer.

As the carpenter son of Joseph and Mary, Jesus spent thirty years in virtual anonymity on this planet. At the appointed time, He presented Himself to be baptized by John the Baptist. The Holy Spirit came upon Him to equip Him, and His priesthood on our behalf began. He journeyed into the desert to do battle with Satan. Emerging victorious, Jesus re-entered civilization. He came to the synagogue in Nazareth, sat down, and opened the Scriptures to announce His ministry.

He did not read that He came to take away the sins of the world. He did not read that He came to open the gates of heaven on our behalf. He did not read that He came to conquer the grave. Instead, He quoted the incredible words from Isaiah 61. He did not quote the entire passage, and I do not know why. For our purpose, I will quote it more fully. Even though what Jesus read clearly communicates His mission of comfort, I want you to gain a more complete understanding of the heart He has for us and the mission He has undertaken on our behalf.

The Spirit of the Sovereign LORD is upon Me,
> for the LORD has appointed Me
> to bring good news to the poor.

He has sent Me to comfort the brokenhearted,
> and to proclaim that captives will be released
> and prisoners will be freed.

He has sent Me to tell those who mourn
> that the time of the LORD's favor has come,
> and with it, the day of GOD's anger against their enemies.

To all who mourn in Israel,
> He will give a crown of beauty for ashes,
> a joyous blessing instead of mourning,
> festive praise instead of despair.

In their righteousness, they will be like great oaks
> that the LORD has planted for His own glory. (Isaiah 61:1–3 NLT)

Do not pass quickly over those words. When Jesus announced His ministry, the sin issue was not at the forefront of His declaration. Instead, He proclaimed His ministry of compassion. He showed His heart to comfort the hurting and set free those in bondage. He affirmed that He came to minister through His presence and not just His promises, to offer Himself as the Blesser and not just extend His blessings. He offered to enter our painful, devastated, broken, and shattered world so He could be all He is to all we need in the moment of faith. He offered us Himself, so we can find hope to journey in and through the traumas we have encountered in our lives.

More Powerful Than Pain

Hope. Without it, we are lost to the seeming omnipotence of despair. The American sociologist Lewis Mumford wrote in *The Conduct of Life* (1951): "Without food man can survive for barely thirty days; without water for little more than three days; without air hardly for more than three minutes: but without hope he might destroy himself in an even shorter time."

Hope is more powerful than pain. Its multifaceted definitions affirm to our mind and heart the glorious power it provides. Hope can be defined as "anticipation, expectation, or aspiration." Hope communicates that we can look forward, that there is potential to be delivered from where we are and brought to where we desire to be. Hope can also be defined as "to believe." Overwhelming pain can rob us of faith, but hope can restore our faith.

This holds true with the word for *hope* found in the Bible, *elpidos*. It is not used to communicate a pipe dream: "I hope I win the lottery!" No, it is a word of confident assurance (Hebrews 6:19). It communicates that our hope is going to be fulfilled—because it is based on the promise of God. Hope, as used in Scripture, is the communication of that which is guaranteed, because God Himself is going to fulfill the promise of hope that He has extended to us.

A Guide to Hope

Until that hope is realized, it is still an issue of faith. Though many think otherwise, faith is actually an issue of sight. Faith always has an object, and for many of us, our eyes are fixed on our hurt instead of on God. Pain is so painful it can be hard for us to see anything else. The loss we experience has a way of making hope a difficult thing to lay hold of. We need someone, who has had their own hope fulfilled, to step into our lives with the voice of experience. They must have moved forward in their own journey of agony. In the darkest days of my own plunge into despair, such a man came into my life.

Having journeyed down his own path of pain, he was able to journey with me in mine. He did not try to fix me. He did not try to lessen my struggle. He embraced me, loved me, and affirmed the genuineness of the agony I was experiencing. Though his compassion did not provide relief, it birthed a glimmer of hope deep inside me. I felt a faint flicker of exhilaration that I had finally found someone who grasped what I was going through.

But he did not stop there. Once he stepped into my world in a way that affirmed his understanding of my plight, he ever so gently encouraged me to believe what I was experiencing was not the end of my story. It was a comma in my journey. My story was still being written and, though my wounds were darkening my world, light was shining bright behind the ominous clouds. He promised that, if I chose to invite God into my pain and trust Him to walk with me in my journey, one day the light behind those clouds would break through and illuminate my path once again.

He spoke the truth! I affirm today the magnitude of his words. It did not happen on my timetable, and by no means were those days easy. As I made the commitment to trudge through the emptiness in my soul with faith in God, the journey was difficult. In many ways the journey is still difficult. In faithful response to my faith in Him, I found freedom from most of my pain. Some of the pain, however, remains. It may very well continue until I see Him face to face, but its present-tense sting is met by a more powerful present-tense Savior.

Radical Freedom

What surprised me, overwhelmed me, and transformed me was that I was able to find freedom *in* the pain. To hurt horribly, with pain that can cause tears to stream down our cheeks, and yet at the same time experience the joy, peace, love, and hope God provides, can only be described as radical. It is otherworldly. Supernatural. Only God can offer this, and dare I even express these words? It is sufficient to encourage and empower us to continue our journey with pain as our constant companion. Radical, indeed.

God has assured us that He will be all He is to all we need, as we journey with Him through our sorrowful struggles (Philippians 4:13). I have walked this path and found it to be true. I have journeyed with others, and they have also found Him faithful to fulfill His promise.

The journey we will go on in this book will not be easy, but it will be honest. We will not shirk the issues, nor seek to come up with pat answers or faulty explanations for your experience. We will seek Him, and that is what will make this a journey worth taking. He promises to be found by those who seek. As you find Him, He will lead you into hope that your own story is still being written. May both the journey and the ending of your story be filled with the peace that God says, "surpasses all understanding" (Philippians 4:7 NKJV).

May the depths of your soul experience what David said can be ours when we put our hand in the hand of our Shepherd God:

He will make you lie down in green pastures and lead you beside still waters.

He will restore your soul.

He will lead you in the paths of righteousness.

You will walk through this, your valley with its shadow of death hanging over you.

For He will be with you, comfort you and strengthen you.

You will enjoy the feast He has prepared for you.

You will enjoy that feast, even as the faces of your fiercest enemies sneer at you;

because His goodness and mercy will pursue you every day of your life, until your earthly journey ends.

You will forever leave behind the painful valleys of this world to dwell completely in peace and comfort, face to face with Him for all eternity in His kingdom, where there are no more tears and no more pain. (Psalm 23, my paraphrase)

This can be your own story!

- CHAPTER 2 -

The Normal
Response to Pain

No one likes to experience pain unless they have deep psychological problems. Our natural human instinct is to run from pain as fast as we can. If you have ever touched a hot pan or frayed wire, you reacted instantly. The extreme heat or shocking surge of electricity caused you to recoil. This universal response is an effort to protect ourselves, in order to survive.

For forty years of ministry, as I have observed devastating circumstances invade the lives of so many dear people, I have seen this absolutely normal response of recoiling from pain. I have watched them desperately seek to withdraw from those circumstances to protect themselves. And I have sought to do the same.

Though the faces have been varied and the circumstances unique, they utter the communally heartfelt cry: "No. No! Please, God, no!" In that cry they are seeking to deny, to remove this horrible circumstance that has crushed them in an instant. Their words pour forth with a faint hope that somehow, someway what they have just heard might not be true. They hope against hope the dreadful announcement that has just pierced their soul might be a mistake. That maybe those words were meant for someone else.

Feeble Attempt

Their eyes perform this feeble attempt at denial. They scan the room, frantically darting to and fro, searching the faces of friends, those dear ones who have assembled to somehow comfort after the merciless blow. They hope to find someone, anyone who might affirm the glimmer of hope that still resides within their heart: "Tell me it's not true!" But the faces sadly confirm that what has been spoken is now fact. A brutal, unavoidable, devastating fact.

The denial remains, and the agonizing cry is repeated: "No. No. Please, God, no." As the words continue, the faces of friends refuse to change, and the faint hope rapidly fades away. The sobering reality sets in, their cry continues—but now in a muffled, almost inaudible tone: "No . . . No . . . Please, God . . . No." The softening of the repeated words reveals that their mind is capitulating to that which can never be altered.

Ever so quickly, the heart receives what the mind has embraced, and the tears begin to flow, rapidly giving way to heaving sobs of gut-wrenching agony. The words are unable to come now as the devastated heart and mind affirm that which cannot be denied. Grief has arrived in all its relentless, soul-pounding waves of agony. It hurts. And it hurts *bad*.

For some, the denial may extend for some time, as if denial has become a friend and comforter. After all, it is readily available to us and helps us avoid the reality of those painful circumstances. And maybe if we stay in denial long enough, the pain will go away. As I struggled with some painful events in my life, I often found myself writing different scripts in my mind for those events. My imagination would rewrite those events with much different scenarios and better endings in a feeble attempt to deny what had happened. Sadly, no matter what fantasy I created in my mind, those fantasies could never change the actual events that happened.

The Haunting Question

At the root of denial is the haunting question of *how*. How could this have happened to me? How could they have done what they did? What they did is so out of character.

When we encounter pain, especially at the hands of others, it comes with the power to shatter our faulty belief that we live in a good world, filled with good people and good circumstances. This belief needs to be shattered because it does not line up with what the Bible teaches. Not only does the Bible teach that the world we live in is under a curse, but it also clearly states that our world is filled with people who have not yet come to faith in Jesus and been transformed into vessels of His life and love. These people are defined in Ephesians 2:1–3 as "sons of disobedience," who are dead in their sins and walk according to the evil prince of this world. If we really believe this, we would not be shocked when we see the evening news reporting four murders in our city today. We would be shocked that there were *only* four—not fifty.

People have incredible potential to hurt one another. Even those who have come to faith in Christ have the ability to make horrible choices when they are tempted by the Evil One to participate in his evil deeds. Jesus made this issue clear when He provided us with His own honest appraisal of our fallen world. He said, "In the world you will have tribulation" (John 16:33). We must embrace the honesty Jesus gave us and, as the apostle Peter stated, we should not be surprised when bad things happen (1 Peter 4:12).

Being a Realist

I do not share this because I want you to become a pessimist. As believers, we remember that Jesus also said to be of good cheer because He has overcome this world (John 16:33). His clear and powerful affirmation to our hearts is that because He has overcome this world, we will too. No believer should ever be a pessimist, especially when we have a Savior Who has conquered sin and death. Neither should a believer be an optimist, whose illusion of a struggle free life will be perpetually shattered in this sin-cursed world. We must be realists, people who are honest with themselves and others. Jesus never promised we would be insulated from the effects of living in this fallen world, only that ours would be the ultimate victory over those effects.

Many believers love to quote from Hebrews 11, how all those

heroes of the faith were delivered from peril by God. Noah built an ark and was delivered from the flood. Moses trusted God to part the Red Sea, and the Israelites were delivered from the murderous Egyptians. Abraham trusted God, and Isaac was delivered from the dagger. These are wonderful declarations of how God intervenes in this world to deliver those who trust Him.

However, believers do not often quote the later portion of Hebrews about those who trusted and were not delivered. They were stoned and sawn in two. They were destitute, afflicted, and ill-treated, forced to live in deserts and caves. Bad things happen in this world, even to the people of faith. Contrary to what the popular song says, this is not a wonderful world. If we do not understand the ever-present potential for hurtful circumstances in our lives, when they occur we will be caught in the perplexing state of attempting to understand how those things could have occurred.

Too Unbelievable to Believe

The tortuous events that came into my life were so difficult to come to grips with, so hard to wrap my mind around, that I could not embrace they had really occurred. My oft repeated cries of *how* and *why* left me stuck in my agony because they kept me in a state of denial. In refusing to embrace my trauma, I could not begin taking the steps to move forward.

I am not alone in this vain attempt to avoid hurting. I had a conversation with a young lady who had endured the trauma of a rape. She shared with me that it took nearly two years for her to fully embrace what had happened to her. In her own words, it was too unbelievable to accept.

Though our circumstances were different, our experience of pursuing an answer for how those bad things had occurred kept us locked in a state of disbelief and denial. That haunting question, "how", wasted years in both of our lives. It prevented us from taking the step of faith to find Jesus, amid our tribulation, as the One Who would empower us to journey through it. Denial can prove devastating because it can prolong our experience of hurt and loss.

Blown Circuits

When trauma invades our body and soul, another wonderful friend and comforter that comes to our aid is shock. Shock is like having our circuits blown. It rescues us from fully experiencing the harm that has come upon us. The dictionary provides synonyms to help us understand how shock fulfills this valued defense against the initial devastation: numbness, bafflement, perplexity, bewilderment, stupor, blankness, and oblivion are wonderful words for those who have been traumatized. The best description I can provide for shock is the "lack of sensation," which is an incredible blessing. Shock shuts down our emotional radar. It insulates us against the pain, preventing us from experiencing the full fury of what has transpired. Without shock, the painful circumstances of our lives could literally kill our soul and our body.

The phrase, "They died of a broken heart," did not just randomly appear in our culture. People coined this phrase when they observed how pain has actually taken the lives of some people. With their souls crippled and their hearts devastated, they simply lose the will to live and rapidly disintegrate until their life just slips away. Shock gives us precious time that protects our hearts from being murdered by our pain. It also provides the opportunity for our minds to process what has happened.

Semblance of Protection

The problem with shock and denial is that they are fleeting. They are not forever friends. They, and the semblance of protection they offer, will wear off. When they do, we will be left to face the grim reality that we must live with this rude, crude invader called pain. The traumatic event crushed us in the moment, but the wound from the trauma can continue to crush us relentlessly with a pain that just does not go away.

When we can no longer deny what has happened to us, the lingering wound becomes our constant companion. It goes to bed with us every night and greets us in the morning. It goes to work with us. It goes on vacation with us. It is with us when we take our kids to the park and to the movies. It even accompanies us when we make love to our spouse. It darkens every day, dampens every joy, and quickly erases every smile. What was once life lived vibrantly now becomes drudgery.

If I am to step back into life, as I must try to do, my attempts at denial must shift into a higher gear. To completely reject what has happened has proved an utter impossibility, so my denial must become more sophisticated. Since I cannot alter my circumstance or remove my constant companion of grief, my only available option is to somehow lessen the loss I am experiencing. Thus begins the search for relief, to breathe again without the sense of hopelessness and despair that comes with every breath. In this thing called life, which feels more like death, I must find a way to numb the pain, to avoid its paralyzing effect on my life.

CHAPTER 3

When You Can't Deny

U nachieved goals, unfulfilled dreams, and hopes that never materialize are constant reminders that we no longer live in the garden paradise God intended. In this fallen world, we lose friends, are let go from jobs, are forced to move away from our families, take pay cuts, and get crippling and debilitating diseases. We grow old, and the list of painful events seems to have no end.

Most of these hurts are like bruises or cuts, which heal quickly and soon become distant memories. Reminders of them function like scars on our physical bodies. Most of my scars are nothing more than physical reminders of pains from long ago. Some of them, though, the more severe wounds, are numb to the touch. Sometimes they offer a weird, tingling sensation, and sometimes they hurt. The physical pain they bring in the present is often accompanied with a brief flashback in my mind of the painful event in the past that caused that scar.

Torn Souls

The more severe hurts cut like a knife to the heart, causing deep emotional wounds. When our trust has been betrayed, when our love has been rejected, and when we have been lied to, these deep wounds may scar over. But when our memory is triggered, these types of wounds can sting and cause tears to fall. Often the memories quickly subside, and life can return to our *new* normal. Sometimes, these painful memories can linger for days, weeks, and even months.

Other wounds are more like gouges or tears than cuts. When they occurred, our souls were ripped open. They cannot be stitched up so easily, and they are not easily forgotten. Some wounds have torn our souls so raggedly that they will never be forgotten this side of heaven. Those deep wounds have the potential to travel through life with us as our constant companions.

Escaping the Pain

Never-ending pain pummels us like a punching bag, forcing us in desperation to find relief somewhere, anywhere we can find it. Because we cannot stop the pain, we must find a way to minimize its effect on our lives. We must find an escape from its attempt to destroy us, even if only for a season, even if our respite is only temporary. At least we will have been provided with an opportunity to catch our breath and, for a treasured moment, stop feeling. We must find a way to anesthetize the scream of agony coming from our souls.

A common method of anesthetizing is prescription medication. These pharmaceuticals can numb or desensitize the pain. These wonderful gifts from God, created by very smart human beings, help us deal with our pain. Sadly, many in the Body of Christ frown on the use of drug therapy by Christians. These frowns are usually accompanied by the condemning slur that anyone who would turn to drugs for relief from pain doesn't have enough faith. In doing so, the condemnation heaps guilt and shame onto the soul of an already hurting individual.

When I hear people so arrogantly despise others who are grieving, I wish I could give them a spiritual slap in the face—in Jesus's name! Not only are they totally disregarding the gaping wound cutting through a person's soul, but they are also completely failing to offer comfort. Their spiritual "counseling" is unbiblical and provides little, if any, comfort to the one so desperately in need of comfort. Such people function just like Job's friends did. They claim to be there as friends, but they function as foes. The New Testament is clear on this issue. When we receive comfort from God, we are to become comforters of others with the comfort we have received from Him (2 Corinthians 1:6–7).

When such people usher forth the call to abstain from anesthetizing medicine, they are not only keeping people from relief, they are also heralding their ignorance of Scripture. Virtually all Christians are familiar with Proverbs 31. The very mention of this proverb instantly calls to their minds the godly woman. Unfortunately, many people so emphasize the godly woman theme of this proverb that they miss two important verses. Remember that the Holy Spirit put these verses into God's inspired Word:

Give intoxicating drink to one who is perishing,
and wine to one whose life is bitter.
Let him drink and forget his poverty,
and remember his trouble no more. (Proverbs 31:6–7)

Maybe you need to read it again to overcome the shock that verse
can communicate to the people of faith. In biblical times, people did
not have our wonderful pharmaceuticals. All they had was alcohol.
Alcohol was the Prozac, Valium, or Lexapro of that time. The Holy
Spirit Himself declared—in writing—that sometimes in this fallen
world our pain can be so overwhelming that we need to anesthetize
that pain. We who seek to help hurting people should provide them
with something to keep their pain from devastating them. If the Holy
Spirit would place such prescription in His Word, who are we to deny
that provision for a hurting soul?

We must advocate for those who hurt and affirm to them
that God permits our attempt to numb the pain that can so easily
devastate us. Though I am in total agreement with this provision, I
must also stress that God's Word also calls us to continue to move
forward in our faith journey with Him, *through* our pain. Because He
offers Himself to us as our strength and comfort, the hope is that
one day we might wean ourselves off those prescriptions as we find
Him to be our provision. In my own experience and in working with
others, very often those pharmaceuticals do not work in the fullest
capacity we hoped they would. For far too many people, the pain
remains, and they continue in their quest for relief and find other
ways to anesthetize themselves.

The Minimizing Method

One of the sneakiest methods people use for anesthetizing pain is to minimize it. People often say something like, "What I have gone through is nothing compared to what you have gone through." This vain attempt to lessen the pain we are experiencing does not work. By focusing on the trauma of another, we never come to grips with our own trauma. When we do that, our wound remains and does what a wound does. It gnaws at us and robs us of the experience of life.

Through this faulty belief system, our pain is masked by a veil of guilt and shame that we should not be experiencing pain in the first place. After all, our pain is nothing compared to the pain of others who have suffered worse. In essence, we are saying we do not have the right to feel the way we do.

Dear one, never, ever minimize your loss and sorrow. Your pain is painful to you. If you fail to admit what you are experiencing, you will never take the steps to deal with it. There can be no cure for a problem you fail to admit exists in the first place.

I will never forget the young lady who had been sexually abused by her father. As she shared her story with me, she did so methodically, with no sign of hurt or anger in her voice. She exhibited a strange disconnection from the tragic events she had experienced as a child. I felt like I was listening to a news anchor rather than a child who had been deeply betrayed by the one who was supposed to be her supreme protector.

When I challenged this disparity between her circumstances and the polite conversation we were having, she quickly offered her "explanation."

"Oh, Pastor Frank, I understand why he did what he did. It wasn't his fault. He was abused as a child too." She was rationalizing and excusing his behavior in an attempt to minimize what he had done. She was trying to protect herself from admitting the horrible reality that her father made the choice to abuse her. If she continued to do so, she would never have a correct and fundamental starting point from which to begin her journey through her pain.

Only when she renounced her explanation and embraced the devastating reality of what her father had done to her was she able to move forward on her journey. It was difficult to see her hurt so badly, but she courageously moved down a road not often traveled. She pursued God amid her grief, and God met her there. She found Him in a way she had never known Him before.

Embracing the truth is necessary and powerful in our journey toward freedom. It is the absolute best prescription for our pain. Truth establishes a firm foundation for us to walk into the presence of God with our pain so He can provide us with Himself. The problem is that so many anesthetics are available to us, and it is easier to anesthetize ourselves than to be honest about our hurt.

Quick Fixes

A dear friend went to the doctor for a complete physical. His doctor said his cholesterol and blood sugar levels were way too high, and he was on his way to having diabetes and heart disease. Lovingly, yet firmly, the doctor told my friend to start exercising and drastically change his diet. Instantly my friend informed the doctor, "That is not going to happen." And then he asked, "Is there a pill I can take?" I trust you see the analogy.

Being honest about our pain is not easy. Deciding to journey with our wounds into the presence of God will be difficult. In our hearts, we are just like my friend. We want an easier way, a pill to take, or a quick fix to make us better. Yet there is no easy way out of hurt. The things we cannot *change* and the things we cannot *get over* are things we must *get through*. Unfortunately, other paths to avoid that struggle never deliver on their promises.

You may recognize some of these "prescriptions for painlessness" as strategies you have used to numb your own pain. These normal pursuits are not inherently wrong. They can be pursued, however, as ways of escaping from reality. They can be a means of living in a fantasy world created in our mind to avoid the hurt. The goal in these pursuits is to so occupy our lives, filling every minute of the day, that we keep ourselves from being reminded of the pain traveling through life with us:

> We bury ourselves in our work.
> We distract ourselves in ministry and service.
> We take every opportunity we can for recreation.
> We dive into books.

We seek to get lost in watching movies.

We find comfort in food.

We become addicted to sex, perhaps the greatest temporary escape from pain.

We shop endlessly for things we don't really need.

We remodel our house, even when it does not need remodeling.

We escape to the internet. This great anesthetic can take our minds virtually anywhere, far away from our pain.

As we seek to escape from our painful experiences, there is no limit to the paths we can choose to avoid having to think and feel about what has happened to us. Sadly, I have heard pastors tell people these woefully inept words, "The reason you're so depressed is because your eyes are fixed on yourself. You need to get a ministry and focus on others instead of always focusing on yourself." Though I absolutely agree that hurting people can begin to obsessively reflect on themselves, doing ministry will fail in its attempt to anesthetize their pain. Just like all other anesthetics, ministry only presents a distraction from their sorrow and will ultimately fail in delivering them. By failing to face the grief and deal with it, it will perpetually abide within them.

Hurt cannot be outrun. Sorrow cannot be avoided. Every attempt to somehow escape pain by sidetracking our mind and emotions will ultimately fail. Pain's demanding scream for attention will be heard. Pain must be recognized, affirmed, and embraced if we are ever going to step forward from its entangling hold on our lives. Instead of fighting against it, we must choose to receive it into our lives. We must never have a spirit of resignation in doing so—but a spirit of resolve that we are going to war and we are going to win!

A Victim's Identity

The traumatic events of life can perpetuate the feeling that we are nothing more than helpless victims. We need to be very careful here. We cannot, and must not, ever affirm the identity of a victim. Victims will never move forward from their victimization because they have embraced an identity that forbids their escape from their painful experiences. When a person embraces the identity of victim, that person never moves forward into healing because that would mean shedding their identity. As a victim, their heart and mind are heightened to the potential of further hurt, and, in an effort to protect themselves, they will build a self-protective wall around their heart.

According to Proverbs 18, that self-protective wall will metamorphose into a prison that they themselves have created. Their wounds function like prison bars that keep people from getting in but also prevent that beautiful person God created from ever getting out. Victims will ultimately function as victimizers because they are unable to receive or give love. In failing to function as a healthy human being, they will forfeit the opportunity to participate in relationship and community. Theirs will be a very lonely existence.

Such people want to be loved. They want to love others. But the fortress of pain that wraps around their heart prevents them from being able to do so. They are like a dog chasing a car. They chase love, but they cannot find it, and if they ever did find it, they wouldn't know what to do with it.

I have seen this played out in the lives of those I have counseled and in my own life as well. By failing to deal with my pain, I functioned for years as a victim. In doing so, I became the victimizer of not only myself but also of those who wanted to love me.

This cycle must be broken, and you as an individual are the only one who can break it. You cannot change what has happened to you, *but you can change what you do with what happened to you.*

This is the path I pursued. I stopped trying to deny and anesthetize what had happened in my life, and made the choice to change what I did with those painful events and memories. I made the choice to trust God in a way I never had before and found Him in a way I had never known Him.

You, too, can make that choice. But that journey can only begin by receiving what has happened. You must put an end to the denial. You must stop attempting to anesthetize as a permanent means of dealing with your hurt. You must embrace the reality of what has occurred in your life and let it lead you to the greater reality that God knows, understands, and stands ready to speak into your struggle. Be aware though that many other voices stand ready to speak into your pain. All too often they do not speak with the comfort and grace that God Himself speaks with. What they say is like rubbing salt in our wounds, and you must be prepared for them.

CHAPTER 4

Faulty Friends with Worthless Words

Christian clichés and pat answers can severely wound those who are already in pain. These well-intentioned words from the Christian community, spoken insensitively, can be very hurtful: "They're in a better place." "God has got this, because God's got you." "Well, you know, all things work together for good!" "Remember what James said: consider it all joy when you encounter trials." These statements are true, but in the moment of pain, the cry of the wounded soul can drown out the voice of truth. The hurting person will lay hold of those truths one day, but in the midst of their hurt and sorrow, those glibly spoken words can pierce the heart like a knife. If well-meaning people sincerely want to help hurting people, they must help in a loving and meaningful fashion.

A dear friend of mine, who recently lost his bride to suicide, shared this incredible word picture. He said the "tactless truth" people spoke to him was like offering saltwater to a dying man. A man dying of thirst longs for water. When he sees people bringing water to him, hope is birthed in his heart that he has found some desperately needed relief. But when that promised relief comes as "saltwater," it is instantly rejected in shocking and even violent fashion.

My friend repeatedly heard these tactless truths: "At least you can rejoice that she knew the Lord. She's in a better place now. You will see her again someday." He embraces this glorious fact, made possible by the finished work of Jesus. But in that fresh moment of pain, his arms were empty, and the house was ominously quiet. These dear people spoke the truth—but without the sensitivity needed to recognize he was too devastated to hear it.

Pondering an Answer

Proverbs says, "The heart of the righteous *ponders* how to answer" (15:28, italics added). He thinks before he speaks. He contemplates not only the words he is going to say, but also the effect those words are going to have on the one who hears them. If we only took those words to heart and practiced them, we could become agents of healing instead of agents of hurt. This is serious business, especially since the rest of that proverb says, "The mouth of the wicked pours out evil things." When we fail to weigh our words carefully, our good words can bring unintended—and wicked—wounds.

I did this recently with a dear lady who lost her son a year earlier. As we greeted each other, without pondering my words, I asked her, "How are you doing?"

She paused and drew a big breath.

Instantly my heart groaned at what I had done. You might wonder what is wrong with that question. After all, it communicates to her that I cared and was sincerely wanting to know the state of her heart. But consider that question from her perspective. How does a parent ever recover from the loss of a child? Their arms are empty, their eyes have no child to adore, and their ears no longer hear the voice of their sweet child. Is it possible to even describe the pain and grief they are experiencing, let alone relate to it?

When I have encountered painful circumstances and have been asked how I am doing, I have wanted to cry out, "How do you think I'm doing? My soul lies in ashes, and my heart is dead right now!"

When our fourth child was born with a rare disease, and her life was hanging in the balance, a friend attempted to encourage me that God was going to get glory from her struggle to survive. Though what he said was true, his statement was utterly insensitive. It was completely disconnected from what I was experiencing in the moment. I offered a very pointed response to him, "Well, how about He gets a little glory out of your child!" My goal was to make him think, which was something he was not doing very well in that moment.

God is too great, our world too complex, and our hurts too fragile to offer such trite responses to someone's pain. Do you see why I recognized in her pause what I had done? Because of my own experience with that question, I should have known better than to ask it.

She is such a kind and precious soul. She did not scream at me. She took that breath first, pondered her answer, and then shared with me that she was doing okay. When we spoke again, I apologized to her for what I had done and acknowledged that I should have known better than to begin our conversation with that question. Our ignorance or insensitivity in this area can add to the hurt people are experiencing.

And it gets worse.

Spiritual Detectives

Sadly, some in the Body of Christ believe they have been commissioned by God as His spiritual detectives. As they stepped into my life, I could almost see the wheels of their minds turning.

"Why did this happen to you, Frank? Let me go to work here and see if I can't help you figure this out."

Then, without any reflection on the effect their words were about to have, they begin their interrogation. "What do you think God might be trying to teach you in this?"

Really? My guts are in a blender, my mind is in a fog, my emotions are out of control with such pain that I am wondering right now if life is even worth living, and you're going to play detective? Where is your compassion? Where is your kindness? Where is your love? If you had even an ounce of love, you would never have embarked on your self-appointed mission to solve this case.

Friendly Accusations

The void of compassion among humanity produces an even more harmful sect of society. These few, who move beyond playing detective, assume the role of prosecutor. As he shared in the foreword, this is what Job's so-called friends did to him. They surmised that, for someone to suffer as Job was suffering, surely he must have had some secret sin in his life.

People in pain do not need such accusation placed on them. Hurting people have already placed that burden on themselves. Most have been led to do so by the Accuser. He is an expert in pointing fingers at us and does not need our help to accomplish his evil plan of stealing, killing, and destroying. Job's friends forgot this. Instead of functioning as vessels of God's love to their fellow pilgrim, Job, they fostered the accusing lies of the Enemy.

If you believe you are to blame for your suffering, please remember that the Holy Spirit's job is to convict you. The Holy Spirit is an expert in this field. Conviction is not something you have to search for. When trouble invades your life, if you have not received that instantaneous conviction from Him, then you have not done anything wrong. This is true for most people who encounter pain in this world. When the Pharisees questioned Jesus about the child born blind in John 9, they asked Him if the child or the parents had sinned. Our Hero and Defender Jesus set the record straight. Neither one of them had sinned.

One sin brought hardship and suffering into the world. It was the sin of Adam. We are told in Genesis that Adam's sin brought a curse into the world that affects every one of us. Romans 5:12 teaches that through that one sin of Adam, all of us were made sinners, capable of committing heinous acts against one another. Further, the Evil One has authority over this world. Man turned over that authority to him when man sinned in the garden. This is a horrific reality that we must understand. The apostle Peter warned us about our adversary Satan, who prowls around like a ravening and roaring lion seeking whom he may devour (1 Peter 5:8). This onslaught against us affirms to us that bad things are going to happen in our lives. Jesus affirmed this reality in no uncertain terms when He told the disciples, "In the world, you will have tribulation" (John 16:33).

The Prosecutor

When our youngest child was born, the first thing my bride and I did was look at ourselves. Through our shared tears we questioned, "What did we do?" We knew God was good, and we knew that as human beings we had all too often failed to do good. We wondered if we had somehow brought this affliction on our little girl.

As we searched this out, we received no conviction from the Holy Spirit that we had done wrong. No sin in our lives had caused our child's illness. We were in the same role as the parents of that blind child in John 9. With the sin issue now behind us, through our tears and the pulsating sorrow in our hearts, we committed ourselves to looking for the glory of God to step into our pain.

We were taking a few steps forward when the prosecutor stepped into our lives. I received the call in the early afternoon, shortly after Avery was born.

He asked the usual questions. "Is Avery going to live?"

I shared what we knew. "No one knows. It is a rare disease, and we do not even know what it is."

He continued, "If she lives, will she ever talk or walk?"

Fighting back the tears, I told him we just did not know. He said he was sorry. I thanked him. And then he defeated the purpose for which he called. Or maybe he didn't.

"Have you considered the possibility of sin?"

I was stunned by his blunt question. I did not know what to say. In typical prosecutor fashion, he offered no other words. He simply waited for a response, a public confession of guilt to pour forth from my lips so he could announce the guilty verdict to his self-convened court. I took a deep breath, and then I broke the silence. I told him he was fortunate this was a phone call. When he questioned what I meant, I did not mince words. I promptly informed him that if he was in my office, he would likely be looking up at me from the floor.

He was now the stunned one, which is what I intended with my strong response. I informed him that no believer should ever ask that question to another believer, especially one enduring great pain.

When people assume the role of prosecutor, they manifest their lack of understanding into what the word *exhortation* really means. Too many people believe that word functions like an accusation, with a finger pointed in someone's face. But the Greek word *parakaleo* means "to come alongside." The heart behind the word is that the *exhorter* puts their arm around the wounded and walks with them as a means of encouragement. It is the same word that is used of the Comforter, the Holy Spirit.

The question of sin being a cause of the pain may need to be asked, but only after having stepped into that person's pain with comfort and love. You earn the right to ask a question like that, or you will be adding pain to the pain that person is already experiencing.

Turnstile Journey

My heart is not to be critical. Just as pain confuses those who hurt, it also confuses those who seek to help the hurting. Since pain and loss were not part of our original design, we lack the ability to respond to pain. Both the one who hurts and the one who seeks to help are ill equipped in their own resources to fully understand pain, let alone seek a way through it. This makes the path of pain a lonely one. It isolates us. No one on this planet really knows what another person is experiencing. How could they? They are not that person. They are on their own journey.

This is true even of those who have walked in pain. They may be able to relate to you better than others who have not endured the struggles you have, but they are not experiencing what you are experiencing at that moment. Walking through pain is a "turnstile" journey—only one person allowed at a time.

The Great Need of a Soul

All it takes is a cursory reading of the Gospels to come to the inescapable conclusion that Jesus's first response when He saw hurting people was compassion. Compassion is the great need of a soul that has been devastated. Hurting people do not need sympathy, which is best described as someone who has pity or sorrow for another. When someone is crushed by pain, it is nice to know that others are sad for them, but it is not enough.

Better is empathy. This rare virtue goes beyond sympathy. It is a genuine and loving attempt to step into the hurting person's shoes and feel what they feel. Empathy is good because it goes a long way toward preventing "tactless truth." If a person can in some way feel the pain of another, they will know better than to offer surface responses to deep wounds.

The danger of empathy is that it is an impossible pursuit. No person can effectively feel what another person is feeling. Even if they have been through similar circumstances, they are not in that moment going through that agony of the soul the other is experiencing. Empathy is better than sympathy, but it is still not enough.

Compassion is best. It is the verb form of empathy. This attitude of the heart compels the will to not only try and feel what another feels but do something about it. Jesus modeled this. We must be careful though, because where He had the ability to fix people's situations, we cannot. Our expression of compassion will be limited, and we must embrace that limitation.

When we walk in compassion, we will not answer a question that a hurting person has not asked. If we really gain an understanding of what they are feeling, we might simply sit down with them in silence. In many situations no words should be spoken—because no words *can be* spoken. In compassion we just hug them and cry with them, as the Holy Spirit suggested in Romans 12:15. The rare virtue of compassion is not usually found on the agenda of spiritual detectives and prosecutors. Without compassion, their attempts to help only bring more hurt.

God Alone

Where can we turn to find someone who can guide us through the pain we are carrying? This is a question that demands an answer. In the Old Testament, a man named Asaph went through an emotional struggle as he encountered the difficult circumstances of life. He was the worship leader for the nation of Israel. His job was to praise God and lead others to praise Him as well. When he pondered his state in life and compared it to the state of others, he observed that very sinful people were prospering, and he was not. As he perceived his lower economic status compared to those who did not honor God, he came to the conclusion that he had worshipped God in vain and that he was in a very unfair place in life.

Many would look at his struggle as insignificant, especially when compared to their own traumatic losses and wounds, but what he was going through was not insignificant to him. The feeling that we have wasted our lives and that life is not fair can rob us of the joy of living. We can become very lonely when we realize that there is no one available or even desirous of understanding our plight and stepping in to rescue us. This is what happened to Asaph.

Fortunately, in a moment of desperation, Asaph looked up to seek God's perception of his unfortunate circumstances. As He cried out to God, He did not get an answer to His dilemma, but He found God was One who understood and had compassion on him. God revealed to Asaph that He did indeed see what was happening in Asaph's life. Further, God affirmed that He would step into Asaph's life to provide an ultimate and glorious ending to Asaph's story. Though his present circumstances would remain, knowing that God would ultimately deliver him prompted Asaph to make this glorious affirmation, "Whom have I in heaven but You?" (Psalm 73:25 NIV).

But then Asaph added a second declaration: "And earth has nothing I desire besides you" (v. 25 NIV). Though no mere man or woman can fathom the depths of our situation, Asaph wonderfully discovered that God knew what he was going through. Coming to know that he was not alone in facing the disparity of a fallen world encouraged Asaph to resume living his life and fulfilling his role as a worship leader. Asaph found that God alone is the One Who will sit down with us where we are until we are ready to walk again. He found that God was enough.

Since God is the One we must find and run to, we would do well to get to know Him. We need to understand Who He is, what His plans are, and how His love and goodness toward us are going to be worked out in a fallen world fraught with evil. The devastating pain and loss we encounter in this world will seek to derail us from understanding and embracing how good and loving God really is. Our grief and sorrow will cause us to cry out, "If God is so good and loving, why am I experiencing this trauma? Why doesn't He protect me?"

Walk in hope and courage as we pursue this together.

CHAPTER 5

The Problem of Pain

*W*hat *if*? has dominated the lives of people ever since man's fall caused a curse on the world. Every day we are haunted by the multifaceted potential for pain that can invade our lives in an instant. What if my spouse leaves me? What if my baby gets sick? What if I lose my job? Fear exists because of the potential for great pain to come into our lives, and no one wants to feel pain.

If you live in this world, you are no stranger to pain. This nasty word is possibly the worst four-letter word in our language. Maybe that is why pain has so many synonyms like loss, hurt, agony, distress, anguish, and the list goes on. Some would say *fear* is the worst word in our vocabulary, but fear does not exist in a vacuum. Fear always has a cause, and the cause behind most fear is the potential for pain. Pain is worse than fear.

Tainted by Fear

When that fear of *what if* becomes a reality, when horrible circumstances invade our lives bringing devastation to our souls, we gain a new statement to carry on our lips: *If only*. If only that had not happened to us, life would have been so much better. The pain of that event parades itself not only into our present but also into our future experiences. Having been deeply hurt, we will be on guard to protect ourselves against future hurt.

We make the choice to only enter into surface relationships and never, ever give our hearts to anyone. We function in life like a lonely island in a sea of humanity. We rob others of the opportunity to touch our lives, and we refuse to intimately touch the lives of others. The consequences of pursuing this path of self-protection creates an isolation in our lives that is more devastating than what originally caused our pain.

By keeping our hurts in the forefront of our minds, life will be seen through the lens of our woundedness. No matter how many wonderful experiences we have, they will be tainted by past hurts and present fears. When I was protecting myself from further pain, I was also missing out on the pleasure life can bring. Coming to this realization, I began a journey to understand pain and find a better way to deal with it. Though difficult to lay hold of, this was a journey worth taking.

Turbulent Love

This issue of pain is a dilemma in a Christian's mind and heart. We know from the Bible that God has revealed Himself to us as our compassionate Father. He loves us so greatly that He sacrificed His

Beloved Son on the cross to secure a relationship with us. Hymn after hymn has been written about this great love that He has for us. It truly is amazing love.

Both Old and New Testaments affirm that His love is beyond definition and beyond comprehension. Ephesians 3:17–19 declares that we can come to know His love, yet that love will always surpass knowledge. Let that reverberate in your head. How can we know a love that cannot be known? The answer is simply that His love is infinite (Jeremiah 31:3), and finite vessels like us will never be able to wrap our minds around that which is infinite.

I once told a group of young people that God's love expressed to us is like placing a glass under Niagara Falls. That little glass would instantly be filled to overflowing, yet that great supply of water would continue to pour down beyond the glass's ability to contain it. In fact, that water flows with such incredible power that it would literally overwhelm and devastate the glass with the power of its turbulence. This is how God loves us—with a turbulent, overwhelming love!

We can never lay hold of how much He loves us. Even in eternity, we will be students of His love. For now, we are left to sing the old hymn in wonder, "Amazing love, how can it be?" with the inescapable glory that we are loved beyond measure. Our journey from the pain that put our guts in a blender must begin with this undeniable conclusion: "It hurts like hell! It hurts so bad I don't know if I can go on! But this one thing I know: God loves me."

Good and Powerful

Further, the Bible tells us God is good. In a glorious declaration from Psalm 119:68, the Holy Spirit testifies that God is good and does only good. Job 34:12 (NIV) tells us, "It is unthinkable that God would do wrong." The Good News translation presents the glory of His goodness in wonderful simplicity: "Almighty God does not do evil; He is never unjust to anyone." We must begin our attempt to understand the problem of pain with this unshakable foundation: God is good and does only good. He has no part in the evil intent and action that takes place in our fallen world.

The Bible also tells us that God is all powerful, that He rules and reigns over the universe. As God, He is actively involved in the affairs of this world, working all things after the counsel of His own will (Ephesians 1:11). He counts the hairs on our head. He knows when every sparrow falls to the ground. He tells us plainly and unequivocally that though man plans his steps, He directs our paths (Proverbs 16:9). God is so big that even though He created us with free choice, our free choice can never thwart His will. Before our minds are totally fried by attempting to understand how this incredible reality plays out in lives, let's pause. We must affirm what we know before we try to lay hold of what we don't know—and may never come to know.

God loves us.

God is good and does only good.

God is all powerful, and reigns over the affairs of the universe.

This is what God says. We must believe what He says or we will never be able to make any sense of this God created, God centered world we live in. Without these stated truths to guide our lives, we will be like a hiker without a map and compass. We will have no starting point for our journey, no destination to seek. Without these affirmations, we will be wandering nomads.

Declare these stated affirmations of Who God is, right now. The Bible says they are true. Personalize them. Stand up and speak them with confidence and determination. These are not just my beliefs. I trust they are your beliefs too.

Left in a Quandary

When we put these truths together and pour that four-letter word *pain* into the mix, we are left in a quandary.

If God loves us, is completely good and does only good for us, and rules over the universe with His Almighty hand that can accomplish anything, why then do I hurt so badly?

How could these evil things that have come into my life and caused me so much hurt, have been allowed to occur in the first place?

Where was He?

Why did He not intervene?

Why didn't He stop these things from happening?

As those questions dominate our minds, we are forced to try to harmonize these contradicting realities in a way we can understand and find some semblance of peace in our soul. When I encounter people who believe they have figured it out, I stand in amazement at their presumptive conclusion. I have been a Christian for over forty years and a pastor for almost the same duration. I have sought answers to those questions myself and heard the answers that many sound-minded, good-hearted believers have sought to present. As I have pondered those answers over the years, some of them have comforted my heart but troubled my mind. Others have satisfied my mind but troubled my heart. Their "answers" have not been "answers" for me. Their answers have left me wondering if there are even answers to these questions. I have little doubt that you have wondered the same thing.

Erroneous Answers

Allow me to share some of those "answers," not to be critical but to be diligent and thorough. In John 8, Jesus declared that coming to know the truth would set us free (v. 32). Because that is absolutely true, and true absolutely, the flip side of that equation is that believing lies will usher in bondage. Truth, by its very nature, must be 100 percent pure or its freeing power will be diminished. Each "answer" these people have suggested brings a large measure of truth to the table. But in the attempt to harmonize what cannot be harmonized, these answers are forced to emphasize one revelation from Father's Word against the other and thus end up being erroneous answers.

Some teachers have built their platform on the greatness and magnificence of the Person of God. They emphasize that He is all powerful and all knowing, as He has affirmed. They herald that no mere man could ever thwart the working of God in the lives of mankind. Through emphasizing His sovereignty over the universe, they conclude that whatever happens on this planet was in line with His sovereign will. Their curt and uncompassionate answer is that whenever something bad happened in our lives, it was God's will. If my brother got murdered, it was God's will. If my daughter got raped, it was God's will. Whatever pain has occurred in your life, it was from God, so just resign yourself to it and get on with your life.

When I hear that dogmatic declaration, my mind reacts and my heart rebels. Their conclusion to exalt the sovereignty of God and not equally emphasize the goodness and love of God has the potential to present God as a hard and despotic ogre. That is not a complete picture of God as He has revealed Himself in His Word. Such a God is certainly ruling over His creation, but that kind of God could never have an intimate relationship with His people, especially those who are hurting so deeply from the consequences of living in a fallen world. If our pain came *from* God, how could we ever run *to* Him for comfort? That would be like a parent slapping their child just so they can comfort that child afterwards. If their "answer" to our dilemma is true, how could we ever trust that God is good?

Many people run from such a concept of God and reject that God. When I hear people reject that concept of God, I believe God says to them, "Good rebel." They are good rebels because they are not rejecting Him, but an incomplete understanding of Who He is. To simply answer that the reason for the pain in our lives is that it was God's will is to provide no answer at all.

Free Choice or a Fallen World

Conversely, some build a foundation on the goodness and love of God. In seeking to understand how tragic things happen to people, their explanation is that God had *nothing* to do with those evils. They proclaim that those horrible experiences cannot be in line with the goodness of God. As we learned from chapter 4, the choice Adam made to sin against God plunged the whole world under the curse of sin and death. Sinful men and women now use their own free choice to devastate others. And this fallen world, which is now under a curse, persistently and perpetually brings pain to our door as a natural consequence of Adam's choice. God did not cause that original sin, nor does He cause the hurtful consequences of anyone else's sin. God has *nothing* to do with the evil that occurs in this world.

At the heart of this "answer" is a desire to exalt, affirm, and defend the stated reality from God's Word that God is altogether good and loving. In doing so however, they are neglecting to equally affirm the magnitude of God's kingdom rule and sovereignty over the affairs of the universe. When I hear that explanation, my mind reacts and my heart rebels. This "answer" is no answer either.

Yes, He is good and does only good. Yes, He loves and only loves. But He is also big and strong. He is also the King of the universe, and He did not abdicate His throne when Adam sinned and plunged the world into sin and death. He is still ruling and reigning over the affairs of the universe. He is still working "all things" after the counsel of his own will (Ephesians 1:11). He is still directing the steps when man plans His way (Proverbs 20:24). When I hear people say that God has no part in the painful events that occur in this world, my heart wants to scream: "Wait a minute! Think about what you are saying! If God is as good and loving and as big as you claim (and He is), then He could have stopped what happened, but chose not to!"

Most people do not want to go there. They will not let themselves hear those words. But we must hear them if we are to be honest with what God has revealed in His Word about Himself. If we neglect His power and sovereignty, we will be presenting an incomplete understanding of God that must be rejected, because *that* "god" is not the God of the Bible. The God of the Bible *is* good and does only good. The God of the Bible *is* love. The God of the Bible *is* also the sovereign King of the universe and rules and reigns over His creation. So how are we to harmonize those stated biblical attributes of God that do not seem to fit together?

Contradictory Realities

We do not harmonize them because they cannot be harmonized. God has chosen to reveal to us in His written Word Who He is. He presents these seemingly contradictory realities to us because in His infinite greatness they are completely true and compatible to His nature and purpose. The problem is that we, as finite beings with the inherent inability to lay hold of the infinite, cannot embrace those stated attributes of God in their totality.

How can God be good, loving, and all powerful, yet allow evil and painful circumstances to occur in our lives? The answer to that question must remain a mystery for us, and we must admit we do not have an answer. Instead of trying to figure Him out so we can put Him into trite formulas and explanations, we need to let Him be Who He is—God.

Some will cry out, "But I cannot wrap my mind around that!" Of course, you can't. You are not God. If you could wrap your mind around that, you would be God. If you could understand the mind of God, God would have a small mind. How pain and evil exist in a God-ordained, God-centered universe can never be understood and explained by us. This pursuit to know all things is a fruit of the lie from the garden of Eden, that we shall be like God. We must reject that lie and give up our desire to fully understand God because we will never be like God. Only God is God, and as God He will forever remain beyond our comprehension.

Though we are in Christ and have come to know Him, He will forever remain unknowable. The finite has no capacity to fully embrace the infinite. If we could understand God, He would not be God. Further, when we try to understand God, there is a great danger that our minds will take us to places they should never go. We must stand on what we do know and not venture into what we do not know. We must let God be God, stop trying to understand what cannot be understood, and be stunned by the magnitude of His greatness. We were not called to dissect Him. We were called to trust Him.

CHAPTER 6

Purpose In Our Pain

We do not have the ability to lay hold of the greatness of God, but the greatness of God can lay hold of us. Consider the depth of that statement. Maybe even read it again. Since delivering ourselves from our hurts is virtually impossible, we must find a way through those hurts. We must find Him as our way through those wounds. Embracing His good, loving, and wise character may be our only answer to the experience of pain in this fallen world. Since God is for us, no opposition will be successful against us (Romans 8:31). Many horrible things in this world can knock us down, but with Him providing His own life to us, those things will not keep us down. He will stand with us and against anything or anyone that comes against us. Let us be convinced this is true and stand courageously in Him when evil invades our lives.

Contemplating God

Our contemplation of God is never intended to satisfy our minds, but to overwhelm us with the incredible glory of His character and power. When we are *stunned* by Who He is, how incredibly good and strong and loving He is, our hearts will bow down before Him and worship Him. In our recognition of His complete greatness and goodness extended through His glorious condescension to us, He will meet us where we are—with all He is—even amid great sorrow and loss.

If contemplating how a good and loving God can allow evil into our lives gave you a headache in the last chapter, this one might make it worse. When discussing the problem of pain and contrasting it with the loving goodness of God, my good friend and brilliant theologian Jim Fowler said some words that rocked my mind. I asked him to repeat them very slowly so I could make sure I heard them correctly:

"God is the essential cause of all things, but He is never the blameworthy or culpable cause of any evil. Evil is contrary to Who He is."

I do not understand that at all, and neither do you. Contemplating it puts my brain into overload. God is the ultimate cause of all things, yet He is not in any way the cause of evil. That sounds like a contradiction. Isn't the existence of evil included in the "all things" that God is the cause of? Since He is good, He could not have caused evil, yet He certainly had to allow evil for it to come into being. How can that be a good and loving thing to do? I cannot find an honest answer that does not rob the integrity of what the Bible teaches about Who God is.

He is good. He is loving. He does rule and reign.

Then why does evil come into our lives when He is big enough and loving enough to stop it?

Secrets Not Revealed

A verse in the Old Testament has brought great comfort to my soul. Deuteronomy 29:29 says, "The secret things belong to the LORD our God, but the things revealed belong to us." God explained His own prescription for handling the things we do not understand. "The secret things," those issues that are too big for our minds to embrace, must remain the secret things. Only God's mind is sufficient to embrace and understand them. We must leave those things to God, things finite creatures will never understand, because they would only cause us turmoil.

The things revealed, however, are a different story. They belong to us. We must lay hold of them and never, ever allow them to lose their place in the forefront of our minds.

God loves us. *This we know.*

God is good and does only good. *This we know.*

God is all powerful and reigns over the affairs of the universe. *This we know.*

God is faithful and will bring all that He is into our lives to sustain and empower us in our journey through this fallen world. *This we know.*

These simple, straightforward declarations from God come to our hearts and minds through His Spirit-inspired Scriptures. He cannot lie. We must believe what He has said to us. As the apostle Paul wrote in 2 Corinthians 11:3 (KJV), we must be on guard to never let our minds be led away from the simplicity of Christ.

In the garden of Eden, mankind lived in simplicity. All they knew was God, and that was sufficient for them. When they rebelled and ate from the forbidden tree, their eyes were opened to *other* than God. They became their own gods. They knew evil and sought to generate their own "goodness" independent of God. They sought to find life in *other* than God. They sought to be in control as God is. They sought to know all things, as God Himself does.

Life for mankind went from simplicity to complexity, which is not what we were designed for. Complexity, by its very nature, cannot produce rest and peace in our lives. A great theologian, Dr. Karl Barth, was once asked to share the greatest theological thought he had ever pondered. Instantly he proclaimed, "Jesus loves me. This I know, for the Bible tells me so!" This wonder of the love of Jesus has been revealed to us and for us, and in this wonder we must rest. The complex things we will never understand must be left in the mind of God.

Though I do not understand, I thoroughly believe what my friend Jim said to me. His words are a summation of what the Bible teaches. We can never explain how God can be totally and completely good and loving, rule over all the affairs of the universe, and yet allow the existence of evil to invade our lives. Perhaps when we are in heaven, face to face with God, God will explain it to us. However, we can illustrate this incredible reality right now, directly from God's own Word.

The Life of Joseph

How can God be the essential cause of all things but never the blameworthy cause of evil? Perhaps the most explicit statement of how God does this is found in the life of Joseph, as recorded in the book of Genesis. His brothers hated their younger brother Joseph, the favorite son of their father, Jacob. With bitterness and resentment in their hearts, they exercised their selfish will. They chose to kidnap and sell Joseph into slavery. He was carted off to Egypt, where he was lied to and betrayed, slandered and abused. Yet God intervened through a dream, eventually using that dream to touch the heart of Pharaoh, who then exalted Joseph to fulfill the role of prime minister of Egypt.

In this powerful role, and in accordance with the dream God had provided, Joseph was used to save the entire nation of Egypt during a time of great famine. In a stroke of irony, he was also able to save his family, those same wicked brothers who had hurt him. Years later, when his brothers appeared before him, bowing to this great "man of Egypt," Joseph revealed to them that he was their brother. Instantly and rightfully, they cowered in fear at what this "mighty man of Egypt" might do in unleashing his revenge against them.

Instead, Joseph recognized and proclaimed how God had infiltrated the evil plans of his brothers with His own plan to exalt

Joseph and deliver so many from famine. Joseph affirmed both the evil intent of his brothers and the good intent of God, in the same circumstance. With great conviction, he boldly declared, "You *meant* evil against me, but God *meant* it for good" (Genesis 50:20, italics added). This incredible insight into the good work of God, in and through the evil work of man in the same event, is the roadmap we are to follow as we seek to make sense of our own painful circumstances.

We dare not make that statement flippantly. We must embrace the language the Holy Spirit used in that passage. The key word in this verse is the verb *meant*, which in Hebrew is *chashab*, meaning "to think or to account." It carries the idea of devising or planning. Those wicked men did not just think evil against Joseph, they put their evil thought into action and executed their evil plan against him. This is exactly what happens to us in this fallen world. We fall prey to the wicked schemes and actions of wicked people who *choose* to hurt us badly.

What we must own in this verse is that the Holy Spirit used the exact same Hebrew word when He described how God was involved in their wicked scheme. When these wicked men were planning and executing evil against Joseph, God was planning and executing—in that same event—His goodness toward Joseph. I don't know about you, but these words prompt more questions than answers for me.

Working His Good

I can hear God is working His good in the evil that men are

working. I can read the words. But I don't know whether I understand what it means. I still struggle with why. Why didn't God just stop their wickedness? If He did so, that would be good too, wouldn't it? If I were Joseph, stopping my brothers in the first place would be a better "good" for me. I would never have been betrayed. I would never have known what it was like to be a slave. I would never have been slandered and would have been spared the pain of prison. But God never asked Joseph's opinion, just as He doesn't ask ours. He simply said that as Joseph's brothers planned and worked evil against him, at the same time He was planning and working good for Joseph in their wicked plan.

Our definition of the goodness of God must include this stunning truth: what looks and feels bad is actually good because He is working His good in the evil we are experiencing. I wonder if His goodness is something we should redefine. Or maybe we shouldn't even try to define His goodness. Maybe the goodness of God, just like His love, is something we can never understand because it is beyond our comprehension. Maybe we are to simply embrace by faith and affirm that God is good and does only good. After all, this glorious "thing" revealed to us, as God said in Deuteronomy 29:29, "belongs to us."

God is good and will accomplish good in our lives. This unalterable fact is from the One Who cannot lie (Titus 1:2). Even though the events of our lives look and feel bad, hurtful, agonizing, and even horrible, God says He is in those events for our good. This must be our full and complete affirmation. We must embrace the inescapable conclusion that there is purpose in our pain.

If you are still struggling with these issues, your pain looks and feels beyond the possibility of redemption, and you're wrestling with how God is ever going to bring good out of your hurt and sorrow, please ponder this incredible revelation from God's Word. In the book of Genesis, God created good out of *nothing*. He is that big, and that good, and that is an amazing feat that our God accomplished.

But in the New Covenant, through the finished work of Jesus, God really outdid Himself. He actually created good out of evil! In Christ, God has made it possible for life to overcome death, and righteousness to overcome sin. It is one thing to create good out of nothing, but it is quite another to create good out of evil. If He can bring good out of our sin, rest assured that He can bring good out of our suffering. He is that big. He is that good. And He is worthy of our trust.

No Stranger to Pain

My dear friend and fellow pastor Ross Gilbert, who is no stranger to pain, has been a source of comfort to me in my own painful struggles. I hope his words will comfort you as well: "If there is no purpose in pain, then God is not good." These powerful words mean that the devastating, gut-wrenching, heart-crushing events of life are not random. Wicked people may hurl their ugly onslaughts against us, but God has affirmed that someway, somehow, He is in their onslaughts with His own good intent and loving purposes.

Joni Eareckson Tada is an incredible lady. After a debilitating accident as a teenager, she has spent her life in a wheelchair and endured excruciating pain because of her injury. Through it all, she has manifested a heroic faith in God. Her affirming words to me years ago still echo in my mind: "God permits what He hates to accomplish that which He loves." Please understand, those words do not satisfy my mind. I ponder why God doesn't just accomplish what He loves without allowing what He hates. But that is one of "the secret things" that belongs to Him, and we are not to force our way into what is rightfully His.

He is God, and I am not. I can never harmonize all He says about Who He is and what He is doing. What I can lay hold of is His revealed character. Our sovereign King is working in all things, even in the evil schemes of this world. His agenda accomplishes what He loves in my life, even when He allows what He hates.

Although those words do not satisfy my mind, they do satisfy my heart. It comforts me to know the painful events in my life are not random. It gives me hope to know they are never occurring independent of God and His purposes. It empowers me to know everything He does and everything He allows is occurring in harmony with His good and loving character. It means there is purpose in my pain—His purpose. And God's purpose is always good, even when it looks and feels bad.

When people are not moved by this affirmation, that God has purpose in pain, it is my conviction they are not in a situation that would adequately move them to it. When a person's life is relatively free of major struggle, they are not haunted by the desperate need to survive. Theological loopholes are easily embraced. The heart and mind are satisfied with an incomplete understanding of Who God is and what He is doing. Only when the soul has been devastated will the magnitude of the greatness of God stand as the only sufficient answer to sustain us through the pain. The wounded heart of such a person knows that God, and only God, can possibly sustain them amid such great sorrow. They must have God, or they will perish!

The Testimony of Jeremiah

Jeremiah's world had collapsed. The Chaldeans had destroyed his beloved city and murdered his beloved people. Smoke from the raging fires stung his eyes. Ashes colored his skin gray as they fell like rain. The smell of death everywhere punished his lungs. Life had turned to death, and he could no longer stand. He sat in the ashes and poured out his heart to God.

Lamentations 3 describes his gut-wrenching story of the darkness that reigned in his soul. No peace. No joy. And worst of all, no hope. He was powerless, in agony, without rescue. With no one to hear his cry, he sat down in the lonely path of pain.

When our world has turned dark and our circumstances do not seem to line up with the goodness of God, we feel alone in our grief. In this frantic state of horror, our minds race for some explanation. The dangerous, desperate flood of raging emotions leaves our minds susceptible to the lies of the Enemy, especially the lies that question the good character of God.

This happened to poor Jeremiah. His pen poured out lie after lie that found its way into his thinking and distorted the character of God. He claimed God had torn him in pieces and would not hear his prayers. He said God was like a lion or bear waiting to ambush him. He claimed God filled him with bitterness and was against him all day long. His stated lies stand against all the Bible reveals about the character and purposes of God, but Jeremiah was believing those lies.

When we believe lies, like Jeremiah did, we will be led away from God instead of drawn to Him. We will be locked in the bondage those lies produce and miss the freedom truth brings. Every lie was an attempt to answer the question of why he was suffering. And every answer was to blame God for his suffering instead of finding God as his remedy.

Amid our desperate times, the thought of understanding why things happened must be banished from our minds. Finding *why* is never a sufficient answer for those oppressed by the darkness of sorrow and grief. *How* must become the supreme question. How will I make it through the agony of such loss? Jeremiah rearranged those three letters, *H O W*, and turned them into *W H O*. He knew in such a deep valley of sorrow that only One in the entire universe was sufficient to come to his rescue. When life has decimated our soul, we must find God to sustain us.

Jeremiah chose to take his eyes off the circumstances of life, reject the lies flooding his mind, turn his eyes toward God, and embrace what he knew about this incredible *Who*, known as his God. He said these words:

> This I recall to my mind, therefore have I hope. It is of the LORD's mercies that we are not consumed, because His compassions fail not. They are new every morning: great is Thy faithfulness. The LORD is my portion, saith my soul; therefore, will I hope in Him. The LORD is good unto them that wait for Him, to the soul that seeketh Him. It is good that a man should both hope and quietly wait for the salvation of the LORD. (Lamentations 3:21–22, 24–26 KJV)

A man—devasted by his circumstances, seduced by lies, and lost in the trauma of turmoil—stopped and remembered Who God was. As he clung to God as his only answer, hope burst forth into his heart and mind that what he was experiencing was not the end of his story. Three separate times in just four verses, Jeremiah cried out that he has hope, yet *none of his circumstances had changed*. He was still sitting in the rubble, covered with ashes, with the smell of death all around him. But he began the journey through his pain, confident that God had a good purpose in store for him.

I, too, began this journey with God through my pain years ago, and you can embark on it as well. As I stated in chapter 3, the journey through pain can only begin by receiving what has happened. We must put an end to denial. We must stop anesthetizing as a permanent means of dealing with our pain. We must receive our hurt, sit down in our sorrow, end the lies we have been believing, and invite Him into our journey.

As I write these words, I can hear the contradicting voices, "But, Pastor Frank, that will hurt too much!" I know, and I understand completely. I have used those same words with my own hurts. Many people in the church echo those words as well. But those words are a lie.

CHAPTER 7

Overcoming The Lies

"More lies are told in church on Sunday mornings than anywhere else in the world." This thought from a friend perplexed me. When he clarified, it made sense: "Think about this, Frank. Why would the Enemy spend his time lying to those he already has locked in bondage? No sir, I am firmly convinced that he works overtime to sow his lies to those who are his greatest threat, the believers. And the best place for him to do that is when those threats are gathered together in church on Sunday mornings."

Erroneous Beliefs

When pain rudely invades our lives, we often create erroneous beliefs about God. "God must not love me . . . He has abandoned me." "God is punishing me." "God doesn't care about me." If we believe these lies, we will never trust Him with our pain. We will never run to Him for His provision in our pain. How could we ever trust Him if we deem Him untrustworthy?

We also form erroneous beliefs about ourselves. We establish these lies in our minds and profess them with our mouths. We believe we are wicked and shameful people who have no significant value, and therefore stand beyond His redemption. Our quick conclusion is that we deserved the pain and are therefore bound to it. Because we assess that we have no value, why would anyone come to our rescue?

The list of lies is as long and varied as there are people and painful circumstances. They are our greatest enemy. These lies we form and believe intensify our pain. They heap shame, guilt, defectiveness, and ill-deserved responsibility onto us. Like a dump truck spilling its full load of dirt, these lies bury us under a mountain of pain we cannot crawl out from under.

Even worse, these lies distance us from God, the only One Who can provide what we need to journey through our pain. If we mistakenly believe He is angry, distant, uncaring, or weak, we will never look to Him for help. Left alone, we face our pain with our own ineffective resources. These blatant lies function like prison walls and keep us locked in our pain until they are exposed and eradicated by the truth.

Refuge and Strength

In Luke 18, the Prodigal Son believed the lie that he would be better off on his own, living independent of his father and doing whatever he wanted to do. Like Genesis says, he was functioning in the lie that he could be his own god. This lie wreaked havoc upon him, and he found himself living a painful, lonely, and empty existence in a far country. He stayed there until he embraced the truth of his horrible circumstances, and also came to realize that his father was good and would take care of him if he went home.

He had to receive and respond to both truths. First, he had to realize he had a problem. If he failed to admit his problem, he would never have gone home. Second, he also had to realize his father was good, and stood ready to help him in his time of trouble.

As we seek to journey from our pain, we must pursue this same path of uncovering and renouncing the lies we believe about God and about ourselves. In their place, we must embrace and act on the truth God says about Himself and us in His Word. The psalmist summarizes what we need to know. "God is our refuge and strength, a very ready help in trouble" (Psalm 46:1). Because this is Who He is to us, we can run to Him no matter how difficult our circumstances may be, even if we are the ones who caused those circumstances.

God declares a call for us: "Be still, and know that I am God" (Psalm 46:10). The Hebrew word for *know* is *yada*, which means to know by intimate experience. As we trust Him to be God to us in our pain, He promises we will know *by intimate experience* that He is our refuge and strength. The truth is a powerful destroyer of lies and an incredible liberator from the bondage those lies produce. We need His truth to replace our lies, especially because the Enemy has a multitude of lies at his disposal. As noted earlier, Sunday mornings in church offer great opportunities for him to dispense his lies.

Too Much

One of Satan's best lies is, "It will hurt too much!" I readily admit that I have never heard that lie taught in church in any formal way. However, I have heard it expressed on the lips of far too many believers in the church. Unfortunately, I have not heard those words strongly refuted by those in the church. The failure to confront this lie is tantamount to affirming it, and it keeps those who are hurt from moving forward in their journey through pain.

I have used these words in my own life. They are contradicted, however, by the glorious truth taught in Philippians 4:19: God shall supply *all* our needs. For years I thought *and taught* that verse was referring to my need for clothing, food, and shelter—the necessities of life. I also believed God could provide by healing my hurt, and I had asked Him to do so. But when I wasn't healed, and the pain remained, I got busy trying to deliver myself through denying and anesthetizing the waves of negative emotions that constantly assaulted me. I never entertained the thought that God wanted to provide for me *in* my hurt.

I was so busy looking for deliverance outside of myself that I never looked inside for Him. He came to live inside us so that He can provide us the power of His own life, which is sufficient to empower us in whatever circumstance we find ourselves in. Sadly, the thought that God would meet my needs *while* I was experiencing grief and agony was foreign to my way of thinking.

If God has promised to meet our needs, then the statement that something can hurt *too much* is a lie. That lie places our pain above His ability to fulfill His promise to us. We must renounce that lie or we will never take one step forward from the painful circumstances that invaded our lives. Jesus said the truth *will* set us free, but the corresponding antithesis is also true. If we believe a lie, we will remain bound. We will be locked in our wound and never be able to receive the truth that we can walk courageously and confidently in that wound.

The truth is that we have a God Who promises to provide His strength for our weakness (2 Corinthians 12:9). Because we are in union with Him (1 Corinthians 6:17), we can do all things through Him. We can walk *through* whatever circumstance we find ourselves in because He will walk through those circumstances with us. When we trust Him and find Him as our supply, nothing that comes into our lives will ever hurt too much.

More Than We Can Handle?

Many churches confidently proclaim another lie that hurts believers bound in their pain. Many will cry out when they experience devastating circumstances that their hurt is beyond their power to endure. Sadly, and erroneously, the church replies that "God will never give us more than we can handle." That statement is a perversion of what the New Testament says.

In 1 Corinthians 10:13, Paul taught that God will never allow us to be *tempted* beyond what we are able to endure because He will provide a way out. This passage is talking about temptation, not painful circumstances. God always promises a way out of temptation, but nowhere in the Bible does God promise that we won't receive difficult and painful circumstances beyond what we can handle. In fact, if we really understand what God is saying in 2 Corinthians 12, God will purposefully allow us to encounter circumstances *beyond* what we can handle.

God permits the circumstances of life to empty us of our strength so we can find His strength instead. God told Paul that the painful circumstances of his life would make him weak, but he was going to be made weak with a purpose. When Paul recognized his weakness, he would cease depending on his own strength. In doing so, he would then look for God's strength and become stronger than he could have imagined. God's purpose and plan for us is always good (Jeremiah 29:11).

Some would be quick to point out that this was a specific purpose intended for Paul alone. But the Old Testament applies this same principle to all humanity. In Isaiah 40, the Holy Spirit wrote that God gives strength to the weary. The young men grow weary, and even the vigorous young men (athletes) grow tired and stumble. It is into this context of weakness that the Holy Spirit added these glorious words: "But those who hope *(braid/intertwine)* in the LORD will renew *(exchange)* their strength" (v. 31 NIV). Because we live in intimate union with God, we are afforded the privilege of exchanging our weakness for His strength. In this great exchange, God affirms that we can "mount up with wings like eagles" and walk in this world without becoming weary.

Life in a fallen world can come powerfully against us, knock us down, and keep us down. But when we look to Him, He will empower us with His own strength. We will then be able to stand and walk through that which has come against us. One of my favorite passages in the Bible is Proverbs 24:16: "A righteous person will fall seven times, and then get up again (NET)." Did you notice that it does not say the righteous person *never* falls? What it does say is the righteous person gets up again. When we fall down, we can get up again. The power of God is greater than the hurtful power that has come against us.

Greater Resources

Pain robs people of their strength. Perpetual pain can steal our joy and destroy our hope. But those who look to God will find Him faithful to provide. He does not offer a renewal of their strength, but a supply of His own strength into their lives. This is what I desperately needed. It is what you desperately need as well.

The pain I experienced confirmed to me that my resources were not up to the demand of what was occurring in my life. I needed resources greater than my own. As the pains of life mercilessly pummeled me to the brink of death, and hope had all but disappeared in my life, I finally looked to God in faith. True to His Word, He was standing ready to meet me in my desperation. He gave me Himself, and He was enough. His grace, His presence in my life, was sufficient, even for the great wounds that resided in my soul.

I personally experienced what the Holy Spirit told Paul in 2 Corinthians 12:9, "My grace is sufficient for you, for power is perfected in weakness." Second Corinthians is such a special book because, in this letter, Paul opened his heart (2 Corinthians 6:11). In the other wonderful letters Paul wrote, we get his incredible, Spirit-taught mind. But in 2 Corinthians, we get Paul's vulnerable honesty, followed by the comfort He received from God in his painful circumstances. In chapter 1, Paul was authentic. He told the Corinthians that the difficult circumstances of life that had come upon him were so great that he was despairing of life (2 Corinthians 1:8).

Paul said the circumstances of life were so difficult and painful for him that he was not up to the demand of such experience. Those circumstances were truly more than he could bear. He described what he was going through as a death sentence on his life. I wonder if he would have been able to share such an honest testimony in our modern churches and Bible study groups. I can almost hear people saying, "But Paul, that is not a positive confession!" I can picture Paul in response saying, "No, it's not. But it is the truth."

Resurrecting People

Fortunately, Paul's testimony continued. He realized God was in the business of resurrecting people who are experiencing death. Obviously, this is not referring to physical death, but the pain we experience that makes us feel as if we are going to die. This kind of pain is devastating. We must understand that our Father God delights not only in resurrecting people from physical death, but also, and especially, from the emotional and spiritual death we encounter every day. God never intends the daily deaths of loss, hurt, rejection, and betrayal to have the final word in our lives. He wants to resurrect us, right now, in those horrible circumstances we encounter, as we look to Him in faith.

In Ephesians 1:19, Paul prayed that we would know by experience the "boundless greatness of His power" that God extends to us. He clarifies that this power is the same power that raised Jesus from the dead. Paul's prayer was that we would experience His resurrection power right now. He spells out this great glory for us in 2 Corinthians 4. This passage has given comfort and courage to hurting people for centuries. I hope what Paul wrote brings confidence to your hurting heart right now.

Paul stated the glorious new covenant reality that we have a treasure inside us. That treasure, of course, is the presence of Jesus. That treasure came to us for the express purpose that "the extraordinary greatness of the power will be of God and not from ourselves" (v. 7). As people who live where painful events lurk around every corner, we *need* that power. Paul stated honestly and affirmatively that in this world we will be afflicted, perplexed, persecuted, and struck down. But with the powerful, resurrection life of Jesus in us, we will not be crushed, despairing, abandoned, or destroyed (v. 8–9). We may get knocked down, but with Jesus living

His powerful life in and through us, we have the potential to never be knocked out.

So That

Paul was a biblical thinker, a realist. He told it like it was. Hurting people need honesty. We are trying to wrap our minds around the events of life that are crushing us, and we cannot do that with illusions, fairy tales, or candy-coated, superfluous clichés. *Tell me the truth! I am drowning and I need a lifeline!* Paul threw us that lifeline. He minced no words. He demonstrated that he was not an advocate of positive thinking, but biblical thinking. He extended to us the shocking reality of what it means to live in a fallen world.

"We who live"—that includes all of us— "are constantly being handed over to death" (2 Corinthians 4:11). When I read those words, I want to scream, "Finally, somebody is being honest about life in a fallen world!" If he stopped there however, every one of us would slip quickly down the slope of fear and depression. That statement does not provide a lot of encouragement. But he continued with some amazing words: "so that." That little phrase provides a reason, an answer, a purpose to our pain. God says there is a purpose for our pain. Death comes at us daily, "*so that* the life of Jesus may also be revealed in our mortal flesh" (italics added).

These are some of the most stunning words in all of the Bible. As the experience of death in this fallen world comes at us from the outside in the form of loss, pain, rejection, and hurt, the resurrection power of Jesus explodes out of us from within. His resurrection power flows from the *inside out*, to overwhelm and overcome the death that is coming at us *outside in*. This declaration of truth proves why the phrase, "It will hurt too much", is a lie. No matter how great our pains and hurts are, His powerful, resurrection life is greater than our pains and hurts.

As you read these words, you might be in such pain that you find them hard to believe. You may be thinking, *But Paul would not have written that if he knew what I had been through.* But in verse 13, he reminds us that we had faith in God before these difficult circumstances came into our lives. Now, more than ever, as the pain invades our lives, we need to continue to believe and speak these words: "He who raised the Lord Jesus will also raise us" (v. 14).

Paul argued here from greater to lesser. His goal was to provide us with the assurance that our pain is not beyond the scope of God's ability to raise us up. If God raised up Jesus in His suffering, which was the greatest suffering anyone has ever endured, will He not also raise us up in our lesser suffering? Like an attorney summing up his argument, Paul was convinced he had led the jury to the only possible conclusion regarding the evidence. In verse 16, he called for a verdict from each of us: "Therefore, we do not lose heart." He raised Jesus! He will also raise us! Therefore, we will stand in His power. We will take a step forward in faith that He will provide. We will choose to live because, though our outer man is decaying, our inner man is being renewed. We are being empowered by the very life of God experienced in us and expressed through us. This is our hope. This is our confidence.

Hope Affirmed

Jesus faced the cross. Great anxiety drove Him to His knees at the prospect of such a horrifying experience. But with the promise that His Father would provide, He courageously affirmed not His own will but the will of the Father, and journeyed to the cross, the grave, and the resurrection.

Paul had such oppression come against him that he despaired of life. In gut-wrenching honesty, he declared that he was afflicted, perplexed, persecuted, and struck down. But because of the life of God that was in him, he was not crushed, despairing, abandoned, or destroyed. He affirmed that the One on Whom he had set his hope would deliver him.

Jeremiah experienced great devastation and personal sorrow. Sitting in the charred rubble of what was once the glorious city of Jerusalem, he cried out to God, recounting the horror he was experiencing. Then he recalled that God's lovingkindness and compassions never fail. He affirmed that God's mercies are new every morning, and His faithfulness is great. Because of Who God is, Jeremiah gained hope that the rubble and ashes of his life were not the end of his story.

Like them, we must not quit. We must have hope. When the pains of life sting us to the core, we must not allow those hurts to have the last word. God is greater than all those things. Because this is true, instead of reacting to our hurt and sorrow, we can respond with faith in God. I pray you will continue this journey into your own experience of hope, that your wounds will not be the last word in your life.

CHAPTER 8

A Radical Response
to Pain

M any people believe their name should be Humpty Dumpty. Since you are reading this book, you may be one of them. You are probably familiar with the old nursery rhyme, but read it again and focus on the power of every word. Read with the intent that this nursery rhyme would burn its tragic reality into the deepest recesses of your mind and heart.

> Humpty Dumpty sat on a wall,
> Humpty Dumpty had a great fall.
> All the king's horses and all the king's men
> Couldn't put Humpty together again. (Public Domain)

As a citizen of this fallen world, I bet you can relate to this dear soul. You were sitting on the wall, just living life, and then you got knocked down. You fell hard and, like an eggshell, your life was fractured into pieces. You cried out for someone, anyone, to help put you back together. But you feel like you have been shattered beyond repair. Your well-intentioned friends, counselors, and pastors tried to put you back together. But alas, they were unable to do so.

Fractured People

Time and again over the years, these fractured people have come into my office for one last attempt at becoming whole again. I once had a conversation with a young rape victim, who had just ended years of meeting with her therapist. When I asked her why she had ended the counseling, she was clear: "It was going nowhere." I gently asked if I could share what I have learned in my own journey, and she agreed to hear me out.

I informed her that my answer would not be an easy one to hear. It was, however, an answer I could give in clear conscience from God's Word, my own personal journey, and what I have witnessed in the lives of the people I have worked with for almost forty years. I believe with all my heart that people want to help us. When people see our hearts hurting so badly, it hurts their own hearts. They sincerely want to step in and see us delivered from the onslaught that pulverizes our souls. But their passion for us and desire to see us healed can be a hindrance to moving us forward in our journey. The problem they have is that they want to stop the hurt. They want to make us feel better. Like all the king's horses and men, they desperately want to see us made whole. I share their motive, but I no longer share their method.

When our lives have been shattered, being made whole again is an utterly impossible pursuit. What happened to us is a fact that cannot be altered, not even by God Himself. I cannot find a single verse in the Bible where God promises to rewrite the past events of our lives. For Him to do so would be fantasy, an illusion. It would not be the life we have lived. God will not do that because He is a God of truth. When it comes to dealing with the ugly truth of what sinful people and a fallen world can bring to our lives, no one can rewrite our history.

Embracing Reality

I told this young woman I couldn't offer a fix or change what happened to her, though I wish I could. I would wish that for myself too. I tried so many times in my mind to rewrite my story, but it is engraved in stone and cannot be altered. Rewriting our story is an exercise in futility and will only leave us frustrated and exhausted. It will also likely increase our pain. Repeated futile attempts to alter our circumstances can rob us of what little hope we still have.

When someone tries to rewrite their story, it is like they are trying to unscramble an egg. It is a pointless pursuit. We cannot change what has happened to us. What we can change is our response to what has happened. Consider the scrambled egg in the pan on the kitchen stove. We were attempting to cook a sunny-side up egg (with an unbroken yolk), but we failed in that pursuit. This event confronts us with a choice. We can stare at that broken yolk in the pan, indefinitely mourning it with an emptiness in our gut, or we can make the choice to do something about it.

Once we embrace the reality that we cannot unscramble our egg, we can resolve to move forward with our scrambled egg. We can add some cheese, onions, bacon bits, and salsa to make some great scrambled eggs. This is what we must do with our pain.

You must first embrace the painful circumstance that has invaded your life. Own it. Stop denying the pain. Stop trying to anesthetize it. Affirm that you cannot run from your pain. It will follow you wherever you go. Boldly and courageously choose to live by faith and renounce the lie that it will hurt too much. Sit down in the pain, even though it may sting you to the core of your being. Then cry out and invite God to meet you there.

Provide God the opportunity, maybe for the first time in your life, to be *all* He is to *all* you need in the moment of faith. He cannot prove to you that His grace is sufficient if you do not afford Him the opportunity. He will never force Himself upon you. He created you with free choice, and He will honor your free choice. Only you can make the choice to trust Him and subsequently, find Him as the One Who can take your scrambled life and make it into something good again. Your life will be forever different, but with your consent to trust Him, He can make life good again. Because of His character, there is always purpose in your pain, and that purpose is always good.

Sitting Down in the Pain

Sitting down in the pain instead of recoiling from it is a courageous step of faith. Many people are willing to take this step with the lesser pains of life. Maybe we got slandered by a coworker or our child was bullied at school or we got in a huge argument with our spouse. These are worthy wounds, and they should not be minimized. They can and should be brought to God so that He can meet us with His provision, empowering us to confidently walk in the discomfort they bring to our soul.

But when it comes to a greater trauma, like the loss of a child, the death of a marriage, or an unwanted divorce, sitting down in that agony and waiting for God to meet us requires a radical step of faith. These devastating realities can hurt so badly, and it can be easy for us to embrace the lie that they hurt too much. When we magnify our wounds to this degree, we are in danger of minimizing God and the provision He offers us in our woundedness. As we face our loss with an impotent god, our pain will seem omnipotent. Left to our own resources, our only hope is that we will survive, but surviving is not living. Surviving is something we should never settle for.

Embracing the devastating traumas of life is a far less traveled road for many people of faith. It has been sad for me to watch so many people fail to trust God with their hurt and miss out on experiencing God in their woundedness. Did you notice in that nursery rhyme that there was no mention of the king? All the king's horses and all the king's men scurried around, but they could not accomplish putting the shattered Humpty back together. Nowhere in the nursery rhyme did anyone cry out to the king to bring his kingly resources into play to meet the fractured Humpty where he was.

Most people who encounter the traumas of life function this same way. Their hurt produces a desperation to find relief. In an effort to escape the pain, in addition to trying to deny and anesthetize their pain, they go on a frantic search to find someone who can deliver them from their trauma. They run to doctors, friends, pastors, and counselors in a vain effort to find someone who can remove the pain. But sadly, just like in the nursery rhyme, they fail to cry out to the King, their Father God, Who alone has the resources to journey with them through their hurt.

As human beings, we see and feel our agonizing circumstances. Pummeled daily by the relentless waves of our wounds, it is easy to fix our eyes on them, especially when we cannot see God. In this very difficult arena, we must make the choice, the agonizing choice, to see God with eyes of faith. We have chosen to put our faith in Him for our salvation. We also need to put our trust in Him for our suffering. As believers, we need to respond to our pain instead of reacting to it. We need to receive our sorrowful circumstances, sit down in them, and believe that God will meet us where we are with all that He is. This radical response to pain may feel like we are putting our hands on a hot pan and keeping it there, but that feeling is not in line with the truth.

This abnormal response to pain is not a masochistic leap into the dark. It is not a decision we make in a vacuum. Throughout His Word, God has promised to be with us and supply us with all we need in whatever circumstance we find ourselves in (Philippians 4:13). If we run from those circumstances or seek to anesthetize ourselves in them, we will miss out on seeing God fulfill this promise in our lives. For years I sought to escape from my wounds, to recoil from them instead of receiving them and inviting God into them. Because of that choice, I forfeited the opportunity to find God as the provision for my wounds. The call to live by faith, trusting the God we cannot see over and against what we do see, is not an easy decision to make. Paul called living by faith a fight, and because the object of our faith is God, it is a good fight (1 Timothy 6:12). Fortunately, others have fought this fight and proven that God provides. The prophet Habakkuk is one such man.

Living by Faith

When Habakkuk was faced with the coming invasion and destruction of Jerusalem by the Chaldeans, he prayed fervently. In answer to his prayers, God told Habakkuk to live by faith (Habakkuk 2:4). This sounds so trite, so clichéd, but only because we are failing to lay hold of the depths of the meaning behind such a call on our lives. We must accurately define what it means to live by faith. The best definition of faith I have ever found is from my friend Jim Fowler. He defines faith as "receptivity to God's activity."

Though it sounds contradictory, faith is an issue of sight. Faith is a vision issue. If your eyes are fixed on you and your circumstances, you will face your pain with your own insufficient resources. You will find yourself wobbling through life instead of standing and walking. God calls us to transfer our vision away from ourselves and onto Him so we can receive Him and then walk down that same path of pain with His supplied life. Faith is our receptivity of His activity. His activity is to meet us where we are with Himself as our provision so we can meet our circumstances with His ability. He promises to be with us, to strengthen and help us, and to uphold us with His righteous right hand so we can face life without fear or dismay (Isaiah 41:10).

Knocked Down

We are so good at focusing on and trying to fix our pain that God often has to get our attention for us to see His provision. I love the way God communicated this to Jacob in Genesis 28. Like Habakkuk, Jacob's faith was verified by God amid great personal trial. Jacob had worked his way to the top. He had gained the lion's share of his father's inheritance through trickery and deceit. Jacob was sitting on top of the world until his deceived brother found out what Jacob had done. Furious, Esau declared his intent to kill Jacob. Fleeing for his life, Jacob found himself alone, a marked man. The Bible records that he had to find a rock for a pillow to lay his head (Genesis 28:11). That is a desperate situation. Are you sleeping with a rock as your pillow? It would have been easy for Jacob to stare at his situation indefinitely, overwhelmed and paralyzed by his circumstances.

Then God stepped in. Four times in five verses God said, "Behold!" Whenever you see that word in the Bible, God is saying, "Change your vision. Pay attention. Don't miss this. I am on the scene. You are not alone." Once God had Jacob's attention, He said, "I am with you and will keep you wherever you go . . . I will not leave you until I have done what I have promised you" (Genesis 28:15). Do you see the glory in what God did? God made this promise to a man who *caused* his own pain. Jacob made the sinful choice to deceive and betray not only his brother but also his father. Many in this world would say to him, "You made this bed of difficult circumstance, now lie in it. You have no one to blame but yourself." But not God!

Our heavenly Father operates differently. How you got into your painful circumstances, and the fact that you failed, is not the main issue on His heart. Because of His great love for you, He is concerned about your well-being. He wants to get you through your pain if you will trust Him to do so. This is our Father's glorious promise, made not only to Jacob but to all who put their trust in Him. Have you been knocked down by this world and find yourself bloodied and bruised? Or have you knocked yourself down by making horrible choices? It does not matter.

God is with you right now, holding you and keeping you, to comfort and strengthen you like no one else can. In 2 Corinthians 1:3–4, Paul proclaimed that He is "the Father of mercies and God of all comfort." He comforts those who are in *any* affliction. Instead of looking for an answer to your hurt, instead of looking for a way out of your hurt, He wants you to look to Him. He wants you to find Him so He can be God to you. He wants to provide you with all that He is to all that you need, in the moment of your faith in Him. He wants you to find Him in a way that you never knew Him before. He wants to prove to you that no matter how great the depths of your pain, His grace is greater.

When this incredible dynamic occurs, you will become a dangerous man or woman in the kingdom of God. They will not have to hear the gospel from your lips because they will see it in your life. The people of this world are hurting. They are in great turmoil because of what they experience in this fallen world. Fear has a stranglehold on their hearts. They are desperately searching for someone who can meet them where they are with honesty and integrity.

When we get honest about hurt and allow our sorrow to be seen, while at the same time experiencing the powerful presence of God, the world will take notice of us. That is why we become dangerous. They will be able to see God empowering us in our pain and perhaps consider that He can empower them in theirs as well. Do the people of this world see this honest dynamic in the church today? It is my conviction that they do not.

- C H A P T E R   9 -

The Faithless Facade

Many believers pursue painlessness instead of the provision of God, causing them to only experience their wounds and not the wonder of God's presence. This inhibited experience of God's goodness leaves them with an emptiness that is not in line with the promise of abundant life. It also places them in stark contrast with the rest of the assembly, who are not currently walking in woundedness and are enjoying the pleasures of life as God intended.

Pain creates foreigners, those who do not fit with the rest of the community. This is especially true for the spiritual community where the death and resurrection of Jesus brought victory to all who place their faith in Him. In the church, this life of victory is propagated as it should be. An army of victors has been produced by the finished work of Jesus on the cross and in His resurrection. This army He has raised up marches into the darkness of this world to bring the light of Jesus. This is how it should be. The life of hope, power and victory is our great expectation. God Himself has said we are more than conquerors in Christ. However, some will be wounded in the battle between the army of God and the forces of darkness.

Wounded in Battle

We will have conflict in our march of faith. A battle creates casualties. Some will get wounded even though the victory has been secured. So where do these wounded victors fit in with the majority who are not wounded? The church must ask this key question and find the answer in God Himself, the same God Who promises that the victim shall indeed be the victor.

The wounded stand in stark contrast to the promised victory. As this glorious army of warriors marches steadfastly into the epic conflict between light and darkness, the wounded lag behind. They struggle to stand, if they can stand at all. Or they walk with a limp and find it hard to keep up. It is my conviction after four decades of ministry that the church, the community of conquerors, does not know what to do with those who are not presently experiencing their victory in Christ. Even if we don't say it, we imply to these soldiers of Christ to hurry up and get better so they can rejoin the fight. These wounded warriors appear to the rest of the community as a contradiction of the victory that Jesus has won over sin and death.

Those who walk in pain know this to be true. They feel the awkwardness when they assemble with the victors. They cautiously wander into the exuberant crowd knowing they do not share in the unhindered praise that emanates from the vast majority. Their soul is bleeding, and they are holding back tears. Many find it hard to lift their eyes, let alone sing triumphantly in their grief.

The wounds they carry can cause them to question if they really are a part of this glorious assembly. They wonder if they will be asked about their pain, sensing that their answer needs to communicate that they are moving forward, even when they know they are not. Even though the realm of humanity gives time for those to heal from physical pain, those with emotional pain are all too often not afforded the same privilege. They have heard the exhortations before, and it will add to their already prevalent hurt to hear them again.

"Are you still struggling with that? That was years ago."

"It's in the past. You need to live in the present."

"You need to bring that to the cross."

"That's just emotions."

But the default phrase with most effective knife to the heart is this:

"You don't have enough faith."

The grief that comes from painful experiences is not predictable. It is not linear. We would like to think that once the wound comes, and we experience its devastating power, we can day by day move forward into healing. That is the way it often works with physical pain. But wounds of the soul are different. They do not heal progressively. This oppressive belief system in the church that we can move on from our painful experiences and never have to face them again is a lie. Pain is illogical. It is not systematic. There is no way to chart pain.

It can disappear for days, and life can seem normal again. And then, in an instant, it can rise up from the depths and ambush us when we least expect it, even with the same intensity that invaded our lives when we first experienced it.

Good Days and Bad Days

This is the new normal for those who endure a fallen world. We grieve over the loss we experience while, at the same time, glorying in the life we have from God, and get to experience with those we love. As noted in chapter 1, we are the only people in the world who can have tears streaming down our cheeks from the sorrow we carry yet still have triumph in those tears. We know triumph because we experience the present joy and peace of our Savior's presence in our lives. We glory in the confidence that our pain is never the end of our story. Complete and ultimate healing is coming for us. In that day, according to Revelation 21:4, there will be no more pain, and He will wipe away *all* our tears. That glorious day, however, is not yet here.

Until that day, there will be good days, and there will be bad days. There will be days that are so bad, we will find it hard to get up, let alone walk. We will find ourselves functioning like David in the psalms, who sings the praises of God and exults with such joy that he can hardly contain himself. Yet in those same psalms, we find this same David soaking his pillow with tears all night long and crying out, "Where are you, God?" Such elation and wonder can exist side-by-side with grief and heartache in the lives of believers.

I once had someone ask me if David was bipolar. I refrained from saying something that would embarrass them and instead offered that David was the total human being. He had both feet on planet earth and both feet in the heavenly realm at the same time.

Note carefully that I did not say one foot on earth and one foot in heaven. That would be double-minded, and no one can serve the two masters of a divided mind. David had both feet on earth. He fully experienced all that a fallen world can throw at him, and he was honest about the struggles he encountered. He also fully experienced all that heaven offered him in the moment of those struggles. As he fully embraced the turmoil in his soul, he also embraced the awe and wonder of a God Who is so great that He can provide all that is needed to walk in and through the agonizing circumstances of life.

The person who asked that question had no understanding of this spiritual normality that we can experience our fallen world and the fullness of God at the same time. That person did not get it, as most of the church does not get it. Bipolar? No, I would call it honesty, integrity, and reality, but most people would prefer not to know such honesty. They would rather live in a world of pretend. "It's all good" may be the motto of the day, but the wounded warriors know that is not true.

Dishonest in the Struggle

Most hurting people find it easier to hide than to be honest about their struggle. Rather than admit a disconnect between their experience and the promise of God, these dear people choose to wear a mask and "fake it until they make it." They wear a smile on the outside but cry on the inside. They present a facade of triumph that is not a manifestation of reality. They parade around as those who never have any struggles. Please understand that no matter how much you smile, that is not true victory. It is conformity, and it will never provide the strength you need to sustain you in your journey. Further, it is dishonest and unbiblical, and a genuinely hurting world will easily see through your facade.

The world is smart enough to recognize hypocrisy and rightly turns away from it, unable to relate to it. Hurting people have no time for a facade. Their loss and sorrow are powerful tools in their hands to root out that which is not authentic. When the church lives in the fantasy world of painlessness, the world sees our failure to be honest about our struggles. Our failure to admit that we hurt causes our influence in the world to remain minimal, and we fail to become the dangerous representatives of the kingdom of God that we could be.

If we would only become honest, admit that we hurt, sit down in that hurt, and find God like we never knew Him before, we would rock the world. Please hear these words. A facade is never powerful, but God is. He wants to be powerful to us in our pain so the world will see Him as the One Who will be powerful to them in their pain.

When this honest faith occurs in our lives, and we find God faithful to us and powerful for us, the world will recognize that we hurt just like them. They will see our tears. But they will also recognize that we have something they don't have. Because we have God working in and through us, they will see the triumph in our tears. As God provides us with strength and hope, they will see us standing up in our pain. And through His provision in our lives, they will see us walking through our pain. Then we will be dangerous people in the kingdom.

When they see us walking with our wounds, they will want what we have because they need what we have. When they see Jesus powerfully alive in and through us, they will want to know Him and experience Him as we have come to know Him, as the One Who saves us right now by the power of His own life that dwells within us (Romans 5:8–10). Their need is the same as ours, to know God in a way we all never knew Him before. The One Who will empower anyone to walk with their wounds, if they would only trust Him to do so.

Jesus would never want you to walk in hypocrisy. While others might see you as bad advertising for His cause, He never will. How could a sorrowful person be false advertising when the founder of our cause defines Himself as a Man of Sorrows? Most people do not even realize that aspect of being conformed to His image. Even those who do see His sorrowful image view conformity to that image as an elective course and choose to not go there. The glory is that you, the sorrowful soldier in His army, are already enrolled in that course. You are already being conformed to His image as a man or woman of sorrows. In fact, you are the kind of person He pays specific attention to for the express purpose of using you as the greatest advertisement for His restorative mission. He came for people just like you because His experience was just like yours. He walked the same path of grief that you are walking.

The Same Path

As a man or woman of sorrows, you are the one in His army who is most like Him. You are traveling the same path of pain that He Himself did. In doing so, you have found Him to be the only source Who can empower you to stand in your pain. The only One Who can encourage you to walk once again with your pain. As He shines His light in and through you, He plays His beautiful song of redemption through you. You are presenting an authentic Savior to a world of hurting people who desperately need to find Him in the way you have found Him.

Do you see how you are a dangerous person in the kingdom of God? You have gone through intensive, special training. You are not only in His army, but you are also in His elite special forces. You are one of His spiritual Navy SEALs or Green Berets. With Him strengthening and sustaining you in your own journey with pain, you are equipped to go to the front lines. You can join those who are in the heat of the battle where the Enemy has wrought his greatest devastation. You can sit down with others in their hurts because you know what it means to live in the valley of the shadow of death. But you also know personally and powerfully how Jesus promises to shepherd people through that valley. In you, they can see and find

Him in a way they never knew Him before. In Him, they can find hope, as you have found hope, that the pain and the hurt are not the final word for their lives.

- CHAPTER 10 -

The Poster Child of Pain

When this well-dressed woman first entered my office, Susie's carefully chosen words made her appear strong and confident. She was having trouble in her relationship with her husband, and I affirmed that she was valued and accepted. I asked if she had any explanation for the issues with her husband or her previous relational troubles, and she curtly offered that it was most likely because she had been sexually abused.

After I thanked her for trusting me, she cut to the chase and poured out the devastating details of her childhood. Like a professor detailing the facts of history, she declared that from age four to thirteen she had endured sexual abuse from her father, uncle, brother, and cousin. She continued, like the narrator in a documentary, with how they had taken turns with her for nine long years of her young life.

My soul cried out in horror for what Susie had endured. I took a deep breath and sought to restrain myself as best I could. With all the gentleness I could muster, I questioned her, "Oh my goodness. Did you hear what you just told me?"

She responded, "Of course I do. These are not repressed memories that just came to the surface recently. I was old enough to know what was going on and lived with those memories for many years."

I took another deep breath and told her I had a real problem.

"And what is that?" she asked.

I told her very directly, "My problem is you!"

"Me?" she asked. "What do you mean your problem is with me?"

I informed her that my problem was that she was telling me her story with no emotion at all. No rage. No sadness. Just facts. "You told me these things like you're telling me the weather."

Unmoved, she responded, "Well, like I told you, these are not new memories." And that was all she would offer me. She had unwrapped her painful package, put it in my lap, and was waiting to hear my response.

But how could I possibly respond? Her circumstances were way above my pay grade. What answer could I give? What answer was she expecting? After all, she hadn't even asked a question.

Breaking Through

I asked the Holy Spirit for His guidance and simply asked, "Where was God when all this was happening?"

Her response was firm and immediate, "Well, I guess He was on His throne." Her answer was laced with enough anger that I detected we had broken through a barrier. The door was beginning to open.

"What do you mean you *guess* He was on the throne? Who is your God? Is He weak and feeble and unable to stop the bad things that happen to good people? Is that your God?"

She sarcastically retorted, "No!" But as she did so, I could see the tears begin to well up in her eyes.

I continued down the path the Holy Spirit was leading us on, "Well, maybe your God is the god of the Deists. They were a first century cult that believed God was all powerful. But once He created the world, He stepped back from what He had created and no longer intervenes into the affairs of mankind. Is that your God? Was He just sitting on His throne, shaking His head at what was transpiring, but refusing to do anything about it?"

Again, I received an emphatic *no*, but this time it was louder and sarcastic. The tears that had formed in her eyes were now trickling down her cheeks.

"Well, then, who is your God? And more importantly, where was your God?"

She paused, considering my questions. There was no sarcasm this time as she answered: "He was on His throne."

I asked what that meant, and she responded with a bewildering affirmation: "That means He could have stopped what happened, but chose not to." And then it shot out of her mouth like a cannon, a one-word answer to a question I had not asked. The same word that has burst out of my own mouth so many times. The same word that haunts every man and woman who has put their faith in a good, loving, perfect, powerful, sovereign God. "Why!" she screamed. "Why would God allow that to happen?"

Finite Human Minds

I was not being mean. But neither was I trying to answer a question that cannot be answered. Nor was I trying to defend the reputation of God, something He does not even do Himself. I was leading her to deal with the problem of her pain and how to harmonize that pain with the good, loving, and sovereign God she claimed to know, just as I offered you in chapter 3. My goal was that she would confirm once and for all that what God says about Himself in His Word is true, even when it doesn't make sense to the human mind. My hope was that she would find God in a way that was beyond what she could imagine or understand in her rational mind. That may sound contradictory. But it is not.

We do not have to understand God to be able to experience Him. If our finite human minds could understand Him, He would not be a very big God. We must embrace that He is big and loving and good enough to stop evil from coming into our lives, or we are not in relationship with the God of the Bible. But we must also embrace that

He is big enough and good enough to enable us to walk powerfully and victoriously through the pain that comes into our life. That requires an even bigger, stronger, more loving, "gooder" God than we can wrap our minds around.

This is beyond our comprehension, but it is not beyond our experience. We can experience the glory of all God is, though in our minds we will never be able to comprehend Him. I know this to be true because I have walked this out myself. I want you to understand this glory for yourself.

The Raging Flow

The tears were now flowing freely down Susie's cheeks. Her carefully constructed, theologically dishonest, self-protective wall of denial and avoidance that she had built for herself was rapidly crumbling. As she faced the reality of her hurt, the waves of agony crashed on her soul. Her previous simplistic answers no longer sufficed. She was totally unable to harmonize those painful events with what she knew about God. Her tears gave way to wretched, heaving sobs as she finally embraced what happened to her. I dared not intervene. I just had to sit there and let her hurt. There were no words I could say. There were no words I should say. There were only prayers, and those I brought to the throne room of the King.

I beseeched God, that the power of the Holy Spirit would break through her finite thinking so she would better grasp His incomprehensible love, a love that He Himself says surpasses knowledge (Ephesians 3:14–20; 1 Corinthians 2:9–14). In Jeremiah 31:3, He screams to our hearts that He loves us with an everlasting love. The word *everlasting* conveys that His love never ends. Though the Hebrew word *olam* most often refers to the future, it can also mean "perpetual, unable to be traced to a beginning." His love has no bounds, no beginning, no ending. His love is infinite, for He is infinite. His love is an infinite river that flows perpetually into our finite lives.

I wanted her to experience the "Niagara Falls love" from chapter 5. I wanted her to be filled with the raging flow of God's love to completely devastate all she had experienced that was contrary to His love. I wanted His turbulent love to be poured into her so powerfully that her hurts would be overruled—and her heart so overwhelmed that it would drive her to her knees in adoration. I wanted her to find Him to be enough for anything she had endured in this fallen world. Though she might never be able to find an answer *for* her pain, my hope was that she would find Him as the answer *to* her pain. God wants all who hurt to come to know that He and He alone is the answer to our pain.

A Starting Point

As the wretched sobs began to subside, Susie's heart and mind were ready. She had reached this point only because I had been honest with her. I had shared what I knew—but also what I did not know. We were about to enter the mystery described in chapter 5, of how God can be good, loving, and all powerful and yet allow evil and painful circumstances to occur in our lives. I hoped she would journey into that mystery and find a God Who was so much bigger than she had ever imagined before.

To her question of how God could allow her to experience such pain, I offered the magic words: "I don't know. But if you want me to, I will go on this journey with you." She readily received my honesty and agreed.

Susie's journey through her pain was not easy, as it is with many of us whose lives have been invaded with trauma and loss. The level of willful, devastating hurt others had brought into her life was way beyond the norm. Further, the prolonged and perverse behavior of those who were supposed to be her loving protectors had provided fertile ground for deception to be formed in her mind. Living out of those lies had become so "normal" for her that it took time to see how wrong her belief systems were.

Contrary to popular belief, the desperate need of most hurting people is not seeking relief from the pain. It is uncovering the lies we believe about our pain and dispelling those lies with the truth. Like Susie, if we never embrace the truth about who we are and where we are in our lives, we will never admit we have a problem. If we never admit the problem, we will never seek help.

By fully embracing the painful reality of what those sinful men had chosen to do, she had a starting point from which to begin her journey. It was difficult for me to walk with her through her traumatic memories. Many times, I wanted to interrupt and somehow try to fix her. That would have been tragic on my part. I would have been fighting against God in my attempt to do what He had not promised to do. With her hand in God's hand, armed with the truth of His inspired Word, she had to journey in and through her pain, alone with Him.

Unlike Susie, most people do not need long-term counseling. For almost forty years, I have observed people come to freedom quickly as the truth dispels the lies. The pain we experience from these lies we believe about God is often far greater than our pain from the traumatic events themselves. When we distort His character, we cannot find Him as our true source of deliverance. A false god can never bring us truth or freedom from our bondage. Nor can the lies we believe about ourselves. When Jesus said we will come to know the truth and the truth *will* set us free, He meant it.

Tears of Triumph

Eighteen months later, Susie came into my office for her regular appointment. She had a gleam in her eye, confidence in her voice, and a resolute countenance on her face. She sat down, and announced these glorious words: "Frank Friedmann, I don't need you anymore!"

"Really?" I asked. "Why is that?"

She instantly responded, "Because I know God in a way that you will never know Him."

"Touché, girl." Then I added, "And by the way, I know God in a way you will never know Him."

"I know that," she said.

She left my office that day, almost thirty-one years ago, and has not been back. I have kept in contact with her, and it fills my heart with joy to tell you that she continues in a dynamic faith walk with her God.

Today, if you asked her to tell you her story, she would readily offer it to you. However, she would tell her story in different fashion from how she told it to me that first day in my office. She would not report her story as a weatherman. She would tell it with tears that flow easily down her cheeks. She would be honest about her pain.

There would also be triumph in those tears. Her story would not only be about the pain she experienced in the past but also the Father God she experiences in the present. Her story would exult in the God she found through the hurts she had experienced. She would share of a God she knows intensely, intimately, and passionately. She knows the infinite, holy, creator God of the universe personally. He provides Her with all He is, as she journeys in faith through this fallen world, with her hand in His.

Unique Journeys

Consider her glorious, hard-earned words: "I know God in a way that you will never know Him." Her journey was different from mine. Her pain was different from mine. But we both found God in a way that was unique to us. He personally met each of us in our own journey. He shared His life in such glorious intimacy that it defies description. When we try to communicate how the glory of knowing the peace, love, comfort, and hope of God can be experienced so profoundly amid great pain, there just aren't enough words.

As I ponder my own journey, and how God revealed Himself to me in my anguish, I can only say that it was the most holy ground I have ever walked on. The experience was beyond communicating through mere words. Only someone who has shared that same glory can understand and affirm, "I know what you mean."

As our time together ended, I asked her a difficult question. Honest friendship affords us that incredible privilege. "If the only way to get to where you are now with God was to go through that pain, would you go through it again?"

Without any hesitation, she responded, "Absolutely. I would not trade where I am with God for anything."

But then she asked me a question. "I sometimes wonder, Pastor Frank, did I really have to go through all that I did in order to find God in the way I know Him now?"

My answer came without hesitation. "I cannot answer that. That is way beyond my pay grade."

She smiled and said, "Mine too. But you know, Pastor Frank, I really don't need to answer that. Knowing Him, the way I know Him is enough."

Susie is now a dangerous woman in the kingdom of God. She

"gets" the hurting people of this world, and the hurting people of this world know that about her. They seek her out as one who will understand what they are going through. They know she has something they don't have, and she stands ready to give it to them. What they desperately need is an opportunity to find God in a way they never knew Him before.

Yes, indeed. Knowing Him is enough.

CHAPTER 11

My Journey

A mere ten words summarized my life story. Two years ago, my bride, Janet, found these words at a craft show. She was quite proud of herself for buying me a gift—a plaque. I thought, *Oh, lamb! After all these years together, you surely know I don't like trite Christian platitudes.* Although I did not verbalize these thoughts, she must have seen it on my face. She instantly told me to wait, that I had to hear the story. I was all ears.

When Janet saw this plaque in a booth, it almost took her breath away. She asked the craft lady if it was mass produced from a mold, and the lady said it was uniquely made by her. My bride was hooked and asked about the story behind it. The lady explained how she was sitting at her table, working on her clay, when a thought came to her mind. She thought to herself, *"Well, that is a nice thought!"* and quickly wrote it down. As she pondered the words, she decided to put them on a plaque.

Janet informed the artist that she had made that plaque for me, and in those few words she had captured my life story.

"Oh, so you know what it means?" the lady quickly asked.

Surprised, Janet questioned her, "Aren't you a Christian?"

"No," the lady responded. "I don't believe in God. Can you tell me what it means?"

Janet shared with her the truth written in this book. Then she bought the plaque—and with great anticipation was ready to give it to me. She pulled out the plaque with tears in her eyes, and as I read it my own eyes filled with tears.

The plaque said, "Grace sat down with me until I could walk again."

That is indeed my life story.

My Wounded Soul

Throughout my life hurtful things have been said and done to me that God never intended for me to experience—things that devastated my soul. I know firsthand what it means to be physically and emotionally abused, to be promised care and then have that security ripped away. I know what it means to be sexually abused. My carefully built bridges of trust came crashing down through lies, deceit, and betrayal. I know what it feels like to be rejected, to be misrepresented, slandered, and ridiculed. I know what it's like to be isolated and bullied. I have experienced the intense agony of losing one you love. I sat helplessly on the sidelines as my child fought tenaciously against death with a rare disease. I have wept as another child endured debilitating and uncontrollable seizures. I have grieved as the Body of Christ bullied and slandered still another one of my children. I watched my father die as doctors refused to treat him because they were on strike against their high malpractice insurance rates. And I have made bad choices resulting in terrible consequences, which brought the ominous pangs of guilt and shame. You know some, if not all, of these things. And more. We were not designed for such losses that bring devastating effects to our lives.

As I encountered these dreadful deeds, my days were darkened and my nights restless. My joy was crushed. My hopes and dreams were shattered. My innocence was stolen. I also had to live with the fact that I had shattered others' dreams, crushed their joy, and robbed them of their innocence. It is a universal law that we can only give to someone else what we own. I had encountered death-ministering experiences at the hands of others, and I gave death-ministering experiences to others. I was a victim, who became a victimizer of others by giving to them what had been given to me.

Life for me, even getting up to face a new day, was reduced to drudgery. The overwhelming pain oppressed me continually, and I could find no way out of the valley of death. I tried to hide from my painful memories, but they found me. As ridiculous as it sounds, I would replay those devastating scenes in my mind and attempt to rewrite the script as it had occurred so those things never happened. My attempt at fiction was powerless. The facts could not be altered. My pain remained.

Pain's Pursuit

Since I could not change what had *happened*, I tried to change what was *happening*. I buried myself in busyness to clutter my life and somehow quiet my raging emotions. I worked. I recreated. I distracted anyway I could, but it was all in vain. I could not hide from the knife that had on numerous occasions pierced my heart. The glory of Psalm 139 took on a grievous interpretation for me.

The psalmist told us the Holy Spirit will always find us wherever we go. If we ascend into the heavens, the Spirit will meet us there. And if we descend to the depths of Sheol, the Spirit is there (v. 8). He cried out, "Where can I go from Your Spirit? Or where can I flee from Your presence?" (v. 7). The psalmist derived great comfort from knowing the God Who reveals Himself as our Comforter will always be with him wherever he goes.

In a profound perversion of that incredible promise, pain had somehow replaced the Holy Spirit as the subject of Psalm 139. At least it felt that way in my life. It seemed that if I ascended to the heavens, pain would meet me there. If I descended into the depths of the sea, the tentacles of grief were there to squeeze the life out of me. At the thought of my omnipresent wounds, my cry was not exuberant like the psalmist, but desperate. Is there anywhere I can flee from this loss?

My desperation intensified with my inability to escape pain's tenacious pursuit. I had to find a way out of this punishing agony. I searched for verses in God's Word, memorized them, recited them over and over, but could not find one that brought light into the depths of my darkness. On the recommendation of trusted friends, I bought a multiplicity of books but could not find the truth I needed.

I sought to numb the pain with alcohol, just enough to take the edge off. But I found the edge of that cliff too narrow and its edges too jagged to provide sure footing. Prescription medication turned out to be a roll of the dice. First one, then another, in a vain attempt to numb what could not be numbed.

Well-meaning friends said to set my mind on God and remember that He would never allow anything into my life beyond what I was able to bear. After all, I was told, the Holy Spirit is so trustworthy that He will never make a promise He would fail to fulfill. This left me in a quandary. The wild emotions I was experiencing remained just below the surface. Like a pressure cooker, they kept boiling intensely, continually calling my mind away from God. Pain was like a demanding child that had to have its way. The memories refused to be forgotten. My journey was a roller-coaster ride that ascended and descended, with a minimal ascent and a rapid, overwhelming descent.

Humbled

Finally, I humbled myself. The carefully built facade I had established affirmed that all was well with Frank Friedmann, until I acknowledged that my public persona was a lie. I had told this lie often and tried to believe it. Perhaps if I said it often enough I would not only fool others but also convince myself the facade was true.

Reality, however, is overwhelmingly powerful. It cannot be overcome with fantasy, no matter how carefully we script the illusion of our own making. I don't know how to describe those days. Maybe I was taking a few steps forward only to take multiple steps backward. Maybe I was walking in a circle. Perhaps the best description would be that I was walking in a maze, trying door after door, but never found a way out.

I have always fancied myself a warrior, quick to answer the call to fight for myself. But when it came to the painful circumstances of life, I found that I did not have the resources to stand, let alone fight. Pain has a way of emptying people and leaving them helpless, and helplessness is a devastating foe.

Beyond Myself

As life painfully dragged on, I finally concluded that I needed resources beyond what I possessed. I sought counseling. Since I had learned to not trust people, I went guardedly, sharing only bits and pieces of the events of my life. I was convinced that if I ever bared it all, no one would really understand. I feared that the looks on their faces would confirm the sense I had of being alone. I also feared being rejected. I reasoned that if they came to know who I really was, their reaction would confirm the shame I was feeling. I have come to believe these feelings are epidemic among humanity.

I can hear their cry. *Is there anyone out there who will care for me?*

Anyone out there who can understand where I am and love me enough to fight for me because I can no longer fight for myself? When silence is all that is heard in response, many people echo the woeful words of the apostle Paul that they are despairing of life (2 Corinthians 1:8).

I found myself there in 1992. I was despairing of life. Fortunately, I found someone who heard my words and stepped into my wounds as a friend who sticks closer than a brother. He spoke healing words to me, words of acceptance, love, understanding, and compassion.

As I grew over time to trust him, I shared my story. I started on the surface with the lesser pains of my life, but as he affirmed his love and acceptance of me, I gradually moved to the deeper pains, the ones I had kept hidden for many years. The compassion in his eyes flooded my heart. His words were a healing balm to my soul. He told me that shameful things had been done to me, and I had done shameful things to myself and others. But in Christ I had been made new. And then he voiced those healing and transforming words.

"Frank, you are not a shameful person." In his gentle way, He affirmed to me that Jesus loved and accepted me just as I am, with all my wounds, scars, failures, and fears.

No More Running

As he taught me Who God is and what God wanted to be to me, I decided to stop running from my pain. I made the radical choice to embrace my pain, to sit down in it, and to stay there until I found God. And there, sitting down in my pain, He sat down with me.

I found God in a way I never knew Him before, just like Job did. He did not wave a magic wand. He did not take away my pain. Instead, He gave me Himself to supply whatever I needed to walk through my pain. He added to my pain the experience of an intimate relationship with Him. He offered me His strength to pick me up so I could walk again. He provided me with a deep and abiding joy that nothing and no one can take away from me. I have a peace that cannot be explained, let alone comprehended. I experience His love and continue to receive more of His love every day. His love is infinite, and none of us will ever be able to exhaust His love, not even in eternity.

Over time, I have been healed of so much of my pain. When the painful memories of those hurtful circumstances find their way to the forefront of my mind, I can face them without them breaking me like they used to do. I am no longer a victim of their oppression. Some of my pain continues with me in my faith journey. Occasionally they rise up and sting me powerfully, as intensely as when those horrible events first happened. They remind me that they are still here and ready to cripple me. They will do so if I do not stand against them with God as my strength, and the truth He provides to counteract the lies those memories bring. I no longer walk in fear of those memories. His perfect love has cast out the fear of having to face those wounds alone.

I have learned to not fight against those pains, but instead to use them as a prompt to look to God in faith and find Him as my sufficiency. When those painful memories ambush me, He sits down with me. He stays there for as long as it takes for me to stand up again. When I am ready to stand, He lifts me up and stands with me. And then, as I walk again, He walks with me, supplying all I need to journey through this fallen world. I have found that I truly can do all things as He strengthens and encourages me with His presence in my life (Philippians 4:13). Like Job and so many others, I did not find a way out of my pain, but I found Him in my pain. He is more than enough. I am not alone in this profound experience of God.

Similar Paths

My friend Bobby Price and his bride, Teri, have followed this same path into the sufficiency of God's glorious presence. Not long ago they lost their precious son to colon cancer. I cannot imagine the pain of having to say goodbye to a child in such a way. After many months, I called Bobby to ask how he was doing. He said they were finally taking their first steps out of the valley of death. When I asked him how they were able to do so, he said they realized they had to stop fighting against what they could not change. They had to sit down in their pain until God met them where they were. I was stunned. Bobby and his bride had found the same path through pain that I had found. Sitting down in their pain, they found that God sat down with them until they could walk again.

A short time after that conversation, I talked to my neighbors Joe and Wendy, whose son has severe autism. These great parents have cared for him and their other children in a wonderful way. They came to the sober realization that as they grew older, they would lose the ability to care for him. When the opportunity came to secure his future in a wonderful care center, they made the best decision for him and placed him in that home.

Their mama and papa hearts were deeply bruised and bleeding. When I asked Wendy how they were doing, she said they were slowly beginning to move forward from the hurtful place they found themselves in. She said they came to the realization that they had to just sit down in their pain until God met them there. Again, I was stunned. There was no way out of the pain for Joe and Wendy, but in finding God, they found the strength to stand and begin to walk again in their loss.

Just a few weeks later, I was on the phone with my friend Nico. He has journeyed for many years with the loss of his brother, who was murdered in the driveway of the family home. As we shared together about our journeys with pain, I reminded Nico of what I have shared with him on many occasions. I told him, "Nico, there is no manual for that kind of pain."

The words that sprang from his mouth stunned me in a powerful way. "No, papa," he said. "There is no manual. There is only Immanuel (God with us). Immanuel is the manual!"

Though our journeys have been different, these dear friends and I have all come to the same conclusion. We had no way out of the pain that came into our lives, but God was there. One of the most stunning verses I have ever found is Psalm 18:11, "He made darkness His secret place" (KJV). When we encounter the dark circumstances of life, we can find comfort in knowing that God dwells in darkness. When darkness comes into our lives, He is already in the darkness! As God sat down with us, we each found that He offered no answer but Himself. He met us where we were and sat down with us until we could walk again. As He made Himself real to us, we knew that although life would be forever different, because of Him, life could be good again, as it can be for you as well.

- CHAPTER 12 -

Not Alone

S itting down in our pain is not easy. It is radical. It is foreign to our humanity. We fight against pain. We do not readily embrace it. When I have asked people to sit down in their pain, if their words did not declare it, the look on their faces certainly expressed the thoughts unleashed in their minds. *Frank, what you are asking me to do is crazy! Why would I want to embrace my pain? It is not natural.*

I get that, and I affirm it as well. What I am suggesting is not natural, but it opens the door to the supernatural. When we sit down in our sorrow and ask God to meet us there, it affords us the opportunity to experience God in a way we never could have imagined.

The formidable strategy of the Enemy is to make us think we are all alone, that no one could possibly understand what we are going through. He tries to seduce us into thinking no one will care enough to sit down with us and love us where we are. When we buy into this kind of thinking, we can easily slip into isolating ourselves and become prey to many other menacing lies he uses to destroy us.

The glorious truth of Scripture, however, is that when we sit down in our pain, we will not be sitting alone. In a simple but powerful declaration, God said He hears His people when they call to Him for help (Psalm 34:17). He promised to be *with* us, to help us, to strengthen us, and to uphold us with His righteous right hand (Isaiah 41:10). He affirmed that when we call on Him, we will find Him (Jeremiah 29:12–13). The One we will find is Jesus, Who understands sorrow and grief and promised to be with us always (Matthew 28:20).

Acquainted with Grief

Consider this: God could have saved us from a distance. He is God and can do as He pleases (Psalm 115:3). Instead, He chose to become one of us and live in this fallen world. He experienced hurt, just like we hurt. When Isaiah revealed that Jesus was a Man of Sorrows, he added this incredible statement, that He was "acquainted with grief" (Isaiah 53:3 NKJV). Most Bible translations use that word *acquainted*, and it is a correct definition. It does not, however, fit the power of the context. I am acquainted with lots of people. They know my name, and I know theirs. We know a few things about each other, but our relational experience together remains on the surface because we are just *acquaintances*.

The second most common translation I have found is the word *familiar*. That is better, but still does not capture the intensity of what the Holy Spirit wants us to know about Jesus. I am familiar with my neighbors. They are familiar to me. I wave at them when we are working in our respective yards. We run errands for each other and take care of each other's yards when we are on vacation. We have even taken vacations together. To be familiar with someone is better than being acquainted with them.

Neither of those words communicates an intimate experience. They are woefully inadequate to impart to our hearts and minds the depth of what Jesus experienced in this fallen world. Jesus did not have a surface relationship with pain and sorrow. The Hebrew word *yada* means "to experience intimately, deeply, personally, and intensely." And what do the translators say He personally experienced? *Grief.*

Grief is a good translation, but I fear we have used it so often that we have grown complacent with it. The Hebrew word *challah* means "illness of the soul." Grief is literally an *illness*. This sickness has entered our lives and will likely take a long time to diagnose— even longer to treat. Some illnesses are so stubborn and powerful that they never heal and just have to be managed. Grief is such an illness, a powerful wound that can leave us devastated for a long time.

Enduring such grief that does not go away forces us to search for someone who not only understands what we are going through but also has the experience to walk us through the dreadful experience we find ourselves in. Jesus is that person.

One Who Understands

In Jesus, we have that someone Who understands what we are going through. He personally knows what it means to have long-term sickness in the soul.

He was rejected by those He loved.

He was publicly shamed and humiliated.

He was deceived and betrayed.

He was physically and sexually abused. (Many scholars believe He was stripped naked.)

He was misunderstood.

He failed to live up to the expectations of others.

He was dishonored.

He was slandered and mocked.

He experienced overwhelming emotional distress and torment.

He was an embarrassment and disappointment to many people.

He was considered a mentally disturbed person.

He was spiritually confused at God's silence in His time of greatest need.

He was abandoned by His closest friends.

Jesus, through firsthand experience, is one Who intimately and intensely knows what it means to suffer illness of the soul. His internal wounds were devastating and paralyzing to His humanity. He knows what we are going through in a world that has lost its glory and now brings grief and death instead of joy and life.

A Bruised Reed

He came for hurting people like us. To do that well, He became one of us. He is not ashamed to call us His brethren (Hebrews 2:11–15) because He experienced His own sorrow and grief. Though many people in the world don't know what to do with someone who is in great pain, He does know. Jesus, the Man of Sorrows, will respond to our cries for help. Isaiah 42:3 (NKJV) offers great hope to those who feel abandoned: "A bruised reed He will not break."

In the ancient world, people would make flutes out of the reeds that grew along the water's edge. These reeds were fragile and easily damaged in the carving process. If they were bent or bruised, the reed would no longer be capable of playing music. They were quickly tossed aside so another reed could be placed into service. After all, there was an abundance of reeds available.

People get bruised in our fallen world. They consider themselves forever broken, and others sadly affirm that they are. Like a bruised reed, they believe it best to be discarded as no longer useful. After all, there is an abundance of other people God can use. The Man of Sorrows, the One Who understands our plight, says He will never discard us. He will meet us where we are with all He is, and He will see to it that our lives once again play His beautiful song of redemption.

In Isaiah 42:3, Jesus offered still more hope: "A dimly burning wick He will not extinguish." In the ancient world, people used oil lamps. In a container of oil, they would place a wick, which would burn slowly and provide them with light in the darkness. Once the wick burned down, they would snuff it out and toss it aside. Another wick would be put into place. An abundance of wicks to choose from could provide their need for light.

This phenomenon of being tossed aside occurs all too often with hurting people. When the dark clouds of grief overwhelm their souls, it is hard for them to provide the light of God to this world. To the religious mind, God should simply discard that person and find another who can shine that light. After all, there are many other people He can use. But Jesus said, "I will *never* snuff you out. I will *never* consider you beyond my ability to restore you. I will meet you where you are, with all I am, and your light will shine bright once again."

God is good, and because He is good, He is compassionate to our plight:

"The LORD is good, a refuge in times of trouble." (Nahum 1:7 NIV)

"God is our refuge and strength, an ever-present help in trouble." (Psalm 46:1 NIV)

You can trust Him with your deepest hurts. He is always available to you. In your weakness, you will find Him as your strength:

"Do not fear, for I am with you;

Do not be afraid, for I am your God.

I will strengthen you; I will also help you,

I will also uphold you with My righteous right hand." (Isaiah 41:10)

When you feel alone, know that He is with you and will never forget you.

"Can a woman forget her nursing child

And have no compassion on the son of her womb?

Even these may forget, but I will not forget you.

Behold, I have inscribed you on the palms *of My hands*. (Isaiah 49:15-16)

In multiple places in both the Old and New Testaments, God has promised He will never leave you or forsake you. With your hand in His, He will guide you. He will bring light into the oppressive darkness that has overwhelmed you and paralyzed you. He will take those seemingly unscalable mountains that have frightened you and level them out for you to walk once again:

> "I will lead those who are blind by a way they have not known,
> in paths they have not known I will guide them.
> I will turn darkness into light before them
> and uneven land into plains.
> These are the things I will do,
> and I will not leave them undone." (Isaiah 42:16)

God assumes responsibility to accomplish this in your life. It is not on you to make these things happen. Your work is to trust Him (Habakkuk 2:6; I Thessalonians 1:3). As you trust Him, He will bring life out of death and good out of evil. This is what God did for Job. Remember Job from the foreword? God turned his darkness into light so Job's life could play the beautiful song of God's redemption once again.

Walking with God

Job walked in sorrow and grief. He lost ten children in a storm.

He also lost his house, his financial resources, his reputation, and his friends. In a way, he lost his relationship with his bride. He was slandered, ridiculed, and misunderstood. He found that no one understood what he was going through. No one could come to his aid.

As Job sat down alone, overwhelmed by his pain, he cried out to God for an answer. He did not find God silent, but he did not find an answer for his pain. Neither did he find a way out of his pain. Instead, he found a God so big and good and wise and glorious that he could not comprehend Him. Through the revelation of how "awe-full" God was, Job found he could trust this great God's character.

Job made the incredible declaration that even though he might not know what God was doing, God knew what He was doing. He embraced by faith that it was too wonderful to imagine. He affirmed that even though his significant losses would make his life forever different, God could make his life good again.

Stunned by the magnificence of God, Job cried out, "In the past I knew only what others had told me, but now I have seen you with my own eyes" (Job 42:5 GNT). With a renewed tenacity of spirit, Job proclaimed that he *knew* God in a way he never knew Him before. This is the same Hebrew word, *yada*, used in Isaiah 53 of Jesus's own intimate knowledge of grief. Isn't it amazing that we gain intimate knowledge of the God Who has intimate knowledge of our sorrowful circumstances? What an encouragement to know that God is in such a deep relationship with us, that He is intimately involved in our journey through our pain.

In coming to know God, Job concluded that he was not facing his loss and pain alone. God was with Him to sustain him and strengthen him. God was with him to comfort him and encourage him. God held him like no one else could. Unlike his friends, God would sit down with Job for as long as it took for him to walk again. And Job *would* walk again. He *would* step back into life. He *would* return to work. He *would* have more children, three girls named Jemimah, Keziah, and Keren-happuch (Job 42:14).

Their names were significant. Jemimah means "daylight," signifying that the light of God had broken through the darkness of Job's circumstances. Keziah means "sweet smelling," referring to the sweet presence of God that comforted him amid the death and decay that had been in his nostrils. Keren-happuch is perhaps the most wonderful name of all. It literally means "splendor of color" and was used specifically for the makeup women used on their eyes. Job was once so broken in pain that all he could see was darkness. But he saw a "splendor of color" as God painted the rest of his life to a different conclusion. Incredibly, the Bible says Job died at an old age, having lived a full (satisfied) life (v. 17).

God's Presence

I do not believe Job ever got over the pain of losing those precious children. But by inviting God into his pain, Job found God in a way he never knew Him before. The path he followed is the path we must follow. As we choose to trust Him in our sorrows, we will experience His incredible presence *in our pain*. His presence will fill us with His joy and peace. They will become so dynamically ours that we will have joy and sorrow at the same time. We will cry—but with triumph in our tears.

This experience is supernatural, only available to those who put their faith in God. It can be your experience if you dare to take Him at His Word. He Who holds our todays and tomorrows offers to hold us if we would only trust Him. He offers to write the rest of our stories in such a way that we will dance again in this life. Be radical. Instead of running from your pain, sit down in it, and find God in a way you never knew Him.

- CHAPTER 13 -

The Agony of Faith

The walk of faith is nothing like the euphoric float many portray it to be. Walking through the valley of death into victory is anything but glorious. This gut-wrenching journey requires tenacity and calls us to move our eyes away from what we see to the God we cannot see. It demands that we not focus on the sorrow pulsing in our souls, but believe that God will take the pain and work it for our ultimate good (Romans 8:28). This fight is not easy.

The Holy Spirit told us in 1 Timothy 6:12 to "fight the good fight of faith." That translation beckons us like a rallying cry to enter the fray with great anticipation of conquest and fulfillment. But somewhere in the translation to English, the meaning of the original Greek words became skewed. If we embrace this misrepresentation of the true tenor of what it means to walk by faith, we will end up inadequately prepared for what awaits us. We will be like the men of the Seventh Cavalry who followed Lieutenant Colonel George Armstrong Custer, galloping into the Little Bighorn Valley, unaware of the formidable foes waiting to defeat them. The walk of faith is no walk in the park. If we believe it to be easy, we are in danger of being ambushed by what our faith journey will really be like.

The literal translation from the Greek says, "Agonize in the good agony of faith." Now that is an honest appraisal of what it means to walk by faith in a good God as we journey through an evil world. Would we expect anything less from a God Who proclaims that He cannot lie (Titus 1:2)? The life of faith is an agony. The pains, struggles, obstacles, and fears of this world are real to each of us. They can invade our lives so powerfully and persistently that it can seem like they will overwhelm us. When this occurs, it is easy to put all our attention on any and every resource we have to deliver ourselves from this onslaught against us. Our usual response is fight or flight. This is where the agony of faith comes in.

We struggle to take our eyes off the devastating wounds crushing us. We equally struggle to take our eyes off our resources, even when deep down we know they are not sufficient to deliver us from our pain. Amid this agony, it feels irrational to put our trust in what we cannot see. Nothing is easy about this choice, especially when the despairing pressures of life rage in and around us. Jumping off the cliff of sight to plunge headlong into the sightlessness of faith *is* this agony of faith.

But is it sightlessness? Not at all. We do not jump off that cliff in blind faith. We have something on which we base our reckless abandon. We have the supreme affirmation of the love and care of God. We have the cross. We have the greatest demonstration of love that can be offered to our hurting hearts. In the cross, we see a love that laid down its life for us.

Paul's Argument

The problem is that our wounds can hurt so badly, and the agony from them can scream so loudly, that we fixate on those screams instead of the sacrificial love we know is there. That is why Paul wrote that though we have believed in the past, we must continue to believe in the present. When hurt and pain invade our lives, we need to believe our beliefs (2 Corinthians 4:13).

The basis for this tenacious and agonizing faith is that we have Jesus. Paul presented a clear and decisive argument from greater to lesser. If God raised Jesus from His suffering, the greatest suffering of all time, will He not also raise us up in our lesser suffering?

As Ephesians says, the power that raised Jesus from the dead now lives in us (Ephesians 1:18–20). It is this resurrection life and power that Paul affirmed will raise us up amid the death experiences we encounter in our earthly journey (2 Corinthians 4:6–16). Paul spoke these words, but he also experienced them.

In 2 Corinthians 1:7–9, he told the Corinthians that he was so afflicted and burdened by the circumstances of his own journey that he was despairing of life. I believe many would reject what he said as not being a positive confession. But it was the truth, and Paul was honest about what he was experiencing. And he had more to say.

He added that as He trusted God, the One Who raises the dead, the One on Whom he had set his hope, God delivered him from the danger of death. Paul believed in the God of resurrection power and so must we, even in the moment of our most desperate pain. This is no easy task. How can we authentically experience and express the hurt we see while trusting with agonizing faith in the God we cannot see?

But God

A pattern in our Father's love letter has helped me tremendously in my own walk with pain. In multiple places in the Bible, the Holy Spirit presents an honest appraisal of the difficulties that are found in our fallen world. Then He adds these powerful words, "But God." He calls our attention to the pain but also that God has the final answer concerning it. "But God" places the power and character of God into that difficulty and presents an alternate ending to the story.

"But God" is a dynamic and powerful phrase, but it is not just a phrase. It is not some positive thinking by which we stir ourselves up to continue to fight with all we have against that which is hurting us so badly. No, the Holy Spirit does not use the phrase independent of a context. The Holy Spirit first puts forth the reality of negative circumstances. Then, and only then, does He present God as the One Who stands ready to provide in that negative circumstance.

These two words allow us to be honest about what we are experiencing yet shift our eyes to an even greater reality. In God, we find the provision to stand and walk in the pain. We no longer function as mere humanity—but supernaturally empowered humanity. We get to experience the power of Christ in us, our "hope of glory" (Colossians 1:27). Together with Him, we write a different ending to our story.

Consider these examples.

When Asaph was encountering trouble in his life, he wrote these words in Psalm 73: "My flesh and my heart may fail, *but God* is the strength of my heart and my portion forever" (v. 26, italics added).

In Philippians, Paul shared that his dear friend Epaphroditus was near death, "*but God* had mercy on him" (2:27, italics added).

While being persecuted, Paul wrote, "For even when we came into Macedonia, our bodies had no rest, but we were afflicted at every turn—fighting without and fear within. *But God*, who comforts the downcast, comforted us" (2 Corinthians 7:5–6 ESV, italics added).

I love Paul's honesty. There was "fighting without and fear within." He was enduring hardship, persecution, rejection, and loss everywhere he turned. I have felt that way many times in my life, and if you are honest, so have you. Sometimes the losses and wounds come so quickly and so powerfully that the fear they produce can paralyze us. But Paul did not stop there. Without minimizing, denying, or ignoring the reality of what he was going through, Paul added those wonderfully encouraging words, *but God*.

Fixing His eyes on God, Paul found the comfort of God and

continued headlong into the battle before him. This is glory. Jesus, the living God of the universe, died for us so He could live inside us. We have the power of His own resurrected life flowing through us so we can live courageously, even with the fear, loss, and pain present in our hearts and minds. This is radical. Supernatural. Paul said that because the treasure of Jesus is in us (2 Corinthians 4:6), we don't quit (v. 16). Oh, "our outer person is decaying, yet our inner person is being renewed day by day" (v. 16).

Intense Glory

This is my experience. This is Susie's, Bobby's, Nico's, Wendy's, and Joe's experience. It can be your experience too. But it requires honesty about your pain, embracing that which has stung your soul. It requires receiving Jesus, Who can provide the power of His life to you. He alone can lift you up by His strong right hand, empowering you to walk again through your pain. As He does, your triumphant tears will herald glory to Him. You will stand victoriously and defiantly against that which sought to destroy you (Jude 24–25).

This is glory. God promises "an eternal weight of glory" that is beyond our comprehension (2 Corinthians 4:17). This is radical. It may seem unreal to have such glory in our seemingly insignificant lives, but it is real—as real as the air we breathe.

We must receive glory from God in the context of what God has said about His glory. In Isaiah 42:8, God made it clear that He alone is God, and He alone has glory. He will not let any false gods compete with or rob Him of His glory. However, He will freely give His glory to His kids who trust Him. The glory He gives us is so intense, it will function as an "eternal weight" in our lives (2 Corinthians 4:17). Own this. God will *overwhelm* us with His glory for all eternity, simply because we became His kids through faith in His Son.

If you will trust Him, He will write the rest of your story. He will not erase or rewrite your history. The author of our faith (Hebrews 12:2) will take your horrific pains and struggles and bring your story to a triumphant end.

Our stories will be told for all eternity with praise in our hearts, pouring out thanksgiving to Him Who loves us so. And how will He write our stories? With our tears.

- CHAPTER 14 -

Never Forgotten

The shortest verse in the Bible is also one of the most powerful: "Jesus wept" (John 11:35). The glorious reality is the context in which His tears flowed freely. Jesus was enduring a sorrowful experience. His beloved friend Lazarus had died. The grave had arrived too soon. But Jesus knew He was going to raise Lazarus back to life. If death would be overruled, why did Jesus shed those tears?

Jesus, functioning as fully human, was doing what human beings do in a fallen world. We suffer loss. We get hurt. Our relationships end. And when these horrible things happen, we grieve. Jesus was modeling for us that it is normal to shed tears in an abnormal world. In anticipation of the fall of man that Adam would bring upon us, Jesus created us with tear ducts. They come with a purpose. They are designed to release the agony that invades our soul.

I grew up in a world where big boys don't cry. When I was a young man, I was shamed by my father for crying in public and told that I embarrassed him by doing so. I vowed that day to never cry again. I dammed up the flow of tears that would normally have fallen in difficult circumstances and tenaciously kept my vow. Only when the tumultuous experiences of life hit me hard was I unable to keep that vow any longer. The dam broke, and the tears flowed freely. Fortunately, I had a counselor who encouraged me to stop functioning like a robot and allow myself to hurt. The tears, he said, would be a wonderful return to being human.

When we fail to cry, we store up our sorrow. We carry inside what we were never designed to carry. Grief. Pain. Agony. When we fail to release those powerful emotions, they build up inside and paralyze us. Rather than live with joy and anticipation, we trudge through each day, weighed down by our wounds. Tears are the God-given release that hurting people desperately need. They are a gift from God, and we should let them fall freely, especially with the knowledge that God promises to *never* forget our tears.

The Grief of Never

Never is a strong word. As soon as we hear it, we know what it means, but I wonder if we grasp the dynamic that little word communicates to our lives. I wonder if we use the word too flippantly, without embracing the glory and grief such a word can bring. *Merriam-Webster* defines *never* as "not ever; at no time; not in any degree; not under any condition." Never is a word of unchanging finality. When it comes to experiencing the traumatic events of life, it is a devastating word.

The excruciating pain we experience from deep wounds burns those events into our memories forever. Not ever, at no time, not in any degree, nor under any condition will we cease to remember them. We who hurt know this to be true. Even the best of friends and most loving family members will fail to embrace this powerful dynamic of the human experience.

When a crushing circumstance invades our life, those who love us rally around us in the moment. They pray fervently on our behalf. They drop what they are doing to sit with us. They weep with us. They spend sleepless nights with us. In our traumatized state, we need them desperately. They know that. They have answered our cry for help, and we are grateful to them.

Their world, however, keeps turning. As the days turn into weeks, and then the months turn into years, they move on with their lives. As it should be. They have been given life from God, and they need to live it. What happened to us remains in the forefront of our minds, but in their minds it is different. The busyness of life often crowds out what happened to us, and it becomes a distant memory for them. We must resist the desire to cry out against this. We must not be offended by it for we share their experience, at least, in a limited fashion.

In the moment of trauma, and in the horrible days and weeks that follow, it *seems* like our world has stopped. It has not. We too have been given life, and we must live it. We must go back to work. We must care for our children. We must maintain our homes. We must continue to pay the bills. We must move forward and continue to live. We, however, do not forget, because we cannot forget. Though our lives move forward, our grief moves with us. For us life will *never* be the same. We desperately need this *different* life to be good again, or we will never truly reenter life. That is where God comes in. He promises to never forget our tears. Though others forget, He will not.

The Glory of Never

One of the most precious passages in the Bible, Psalm 56, was written by David. In 1 Samuel 21:10–15, David had been captured by the Philistines. He was alone, desperate, and afraid. Can you relate to such times in your own life? The intensity of the raging emotions within caused him to get right to the point.

I am being attacked! I am being trampled upon! I am being oppressed! I am misunderstood, slandered, and in misery. In such times, our tears flow freely as we search for someone, anyone who will understand and come to our aid. With his world imploding, David chose to have his own "But God" moment. He declared that God not only knew what was happening but also cared about it. Because David knew God cared for him, he assured himself: "This I know, that God is for me" (Psalm 56:9). He chose to believe, as he should, that God would step into his darkness with such power that he would again walk in the light of the living.

As David voiced his confidence in God, God collected David's tears. But He did not just collect them, He took ownership of them.

He put David's tears in His bottle and recorded them in His ledger (v. 8). God has promised that He will never forget our tears—not ever, at no time, not in any degree, nor under any condition. As we continue to carry our pain, He continues to carry it with us. He is truly the Good Shepherd, Who walks with us through the valley of the shadow of death until He brings us into the glorious banquet He has prepared for us in the presence of our enemies (Psalm 23).

New Life

Hidden glory appears in the word that has been translated "bottle." The root of the Hebrew word is *nod*, which is translated elsewhere in the Old Testament as "wineskin." If we translate the word as "wineskin" instead of "bottle," it has tremendous ramifications for us in terms of what God is communicating through this passage.

In the ancient world, people put their newly crushed grape juice into a wineskin. In time, the juice would become wine. Throughout both Old and New Testaments, wine is used as a reference to new life. If this truth is applied to Psalm 56, as it should be, David testified that God stores up our tears in His wineskin. As we trust God with our sorrows, He will, over time, transform those tears into new wine. He will write the rest of our story with the ink of our transformed tears, symbolic of our new life.

In Psalm 56, God announced that our stories will rise up out of the ashes to become epic accounts of how life has conquered death. Our grief will be consumed by His glory. We will have our own "But

God" experiences. Because God is with us, our pain will *never* have the last word in our lives.

This is why I have said throughout this book, there is triumph in our tears. We do not grieve as those who have no hope. We are in intimate relationship with the One Who has promised us that He will cause all things to work together for our good (Romans 8:28), and He cannot lie (Titus 1:2). In Jesus, He has fulfilled all His promises. Sharing in His life, we have His comfort and His joy right now. We have His strength right now, even in our weakness. We have His peace right now!

Because He walks with us as our ever-present help in times of trouble (Psalm 46:1), we will stand and walk again. Though our tears may remain, and continue to flow down our cheeks, there will be triumph in our tears. This is our confidence.

- CHAPTER 15 -

Setting Our Minds

*B*ut God. I pray that this little phrase becomes the mantra of your life. This world is not going to change. If we understand what Paul said in his letters, it will get worse as people move further from God (2 Timothy 3:1). This descent into depravity will provide a rich environment for all of us to endure more painful circumstances. We must be honest about this reality and be careful to not present the idea that Jesus came to provide a utopia. On the contrary, the implication of the New Testament is that, as the world grows ever darker, it will provide greater opportunity for us to shine the light of His love into that darkness. That will not happen unless we embrace God fully so we can experience and express Him dynamically.

We must be honest about our pain to find God up to the demand that our sorrows place on our lives. However, we must establish those two realities in their proper order. My friend Dan Stone gave us a wonderful gift to describe this. He said that when we use "But God," we must recognize that what comes *after* the "but" is what we really believe.

Consider this confession of faith: "God is so big and loving, and I know He is for me and with me to deliver me in the midst of this trial, *but* it hurts so bad I don't know if I will be able to make it another day!"

My first thought, that God is good and loving, has been replaced by my second thought, that my trial is overwhelming. That *negative* thought is the one I chose to hang my hat on. My concluding thought remains and dominates my mind.

Watch what happens when we reverse it: "What I am going through right now hurts so bad I don't know if I will be able to make it another day, *but* I know God is so big and loving, and I know He is for me and with me to deliver me in the midst of this trial."

Now my negative experience has been replaced by the *greater* promise of God. My positive thought, that God will be with me in my struggle, is my concluding thought. I will move forward in my day, embracing that even though it hurts, I know that God knows. He cares for me and will rise up on my behalf.

Whatever Is True

Replacing our negative experiences with God's truth is not playing mind games. It is thinking biblically, something the Bible calls "setting the mind." Throughout the Old and New Testaments, setting our mind is one of the supreme exhortations the Holy Spirit has placed on our lives. To experience the victory God has promised and already secured for us, that victory must be practiced. The way to practice is to place the presence of God in the forefront of our minds.

The Holy Spirit stated in Romans 12:2: "And do not be conformed to this world, but be transformed by the renewing of your mind, so that you may prove what the will of God is, that which is good and acceptable and perfect."

Again, in Philippians 4:8–9, He stated, "Whatever is true, whatever is honorable, whatever is right, whatever is pure, whatever is lovely, whatever is commendable, if there is any excellence and if anything worthy of praise, think about these things. As for the things you have learned and received and heard and seen in me, practice these things, and the God of peace will be with you."

It is one thing to believe God is with us and has promised to never leave us or forsake us (Hebrews 13:5) yet quite different to live daily in that knowledge. This comes through remembering, setting our minds, acknowledging that He is with us. Living it takes diligent practice because many things in life attempt to distract our minds from God. As my friend Malcolm Smith has said to me, "It is one thing to have a thought. It is quite another to invite that thought to sit down for a cup of tea and stay."

We cannot control the thoughts that come into our minds. But we have the power to choose if those thoughts remain there. The key to winning this battle is to not fight against those thoughts. When we fight, we unwittingly keep them in our minds: "I am not going to think about that anymore!" Well, you just thought about it and have already lost the battle.

To win in the war of the mind, we must replace our thoughts instead of fighting against them. We must choose to put another thought into our minds instead of the painful one. Proverbs 23:7 may be the best passage to herald this dynamic. Solomon stated it in a simplistic, yet powerful fashion: "For as he thinks within himself, so he is."

There it is. What you allow to stay in your mind is what will be expressed in your life. If your mind is *set* on fear, you will be fearful. If your mind is fixed on those painful circumstances, you will experience hurt and sorrow. Those painful thoughts of the *past* must be replaced with the *present* presence of God and the hope He has established in our hearts. Those painful memories must be replaced with the present promise of God.

Our present pain will announce itself repeatedly. It will scream, "I am here!"

We must implement our "But God" strategy and scream back, "My God is also here!"

Our Battle Strategy

We must never minimize, deny, or try to forget the painful experiences we have endured. We must face them honestly. Pain must be received, but we cannot let it have the final word. As the wounds of life demand the first place in our minds, with gritted teeth and determination, we will declare our own, "But God." When the memories come, we must use them as a prompt to remind us that

God is with us. We must replace them with the knowledge that the completely good, trustworthy, all-powerful God of the universe is in us. We must affirm that He stands like a mighty warrior ready to provide Himself for us, to battle with us against the one who seeks to steal, kill, and destroy. This is where our minds must be fixed.

My friend Malcolm communicates this well: "Frank, a thought is a thought. I cannot keep the thoughts from coming into my mind any more than I can keep the birds from flying over my head. But I can keep them from making a nest in my hair."

This is our battle strategy. Though we embrace the pain, we do not let that pain make its nest and rule our minds. We must make our own nest with the promise that God will empower us to walk through our pain and arrive at the victory banquet. We are to trust God. In Psalm 56, David modeled how to do this. Though he acknowledged the painful circumstances of his life, David decided and declared twice that he would trust the promise of God to bring Him through his struggle.

"I will put my trust in You," (Psalm 56:4).

"In God I have put my trust," (Psalm 56:11).

My prayer is that you will trust Him too. As you do, He will be faithful to fulfill His promise to walk with you. He will prove that He is greater than your grief, for He is God. Let your tears flow freely, and entrust your tears to Him. Do so with confidence, knowing that every tear that fills your eyes and spills down your cheeks will be captured by God in His bottle. In His wineskin, the One Who "gets it," the One Who cares, will transform those tears into new wine (new life). With Him as your coauthor, you will write the rest of your story with that new wine.

- CHAPTER 16 -

The True Face of Faith

A
s I walked into the intensive care unit, I saw life fighting against death. As it should be. A dear woman in our church had suffered a massive heart attack. Her hold on life was especially tenuous. This single mother of four young girls fought courageously for almost two weeks, but it became clear she would not survive. Her mama's heart was fighting two battles. Through her faith in Jesus, she had secured her ultimate victory and would be with Him in glory. This brought her great comfort. Losing her earthly battle, however, would leave her children without their mother or their father. This inescapable reality brought her agonizing sorrow. I cannot begin to imagine the conflicting, roller-coaster emotions she was experiencing in her soul.

Our church family held a round-the-clock vigil at her bedside, offering themselves as agents of comfort and mercy. We affirmed that, as a community, we would rally around her children and care for them in her absence. Yet the soberness death brings to our world filled the air with heaviness.

As I entered the ICU, one of the women in our church was

coming out of this young mother's room. Tears were streaming down her cheeks. Another woman, who was going into the room, scolded her. "Stop it," she said. "Your tears are not manifesting victory!" The dear lady who made that declaration was emphasizing the glory that we are going to heaven, but she was missing the hell we can live in here on Earth.

A huge misconception had taken place in that room. I met with each of those women individually to address the issue, which motivated me to deal with it publicly. Unfortunately, the mindset displayed in that event are epidemic in the Body of Christ. Though the motives are sincere, they are sincerely wrong.

Manifest Victory

The heart behind the desire to manifest victory is good. Those of us who have found a relationship with God through Christ have recognized the incredible cost of our salvation. We agree with Peter that the shed blood of Jesus is precious, far more valuable than gold or silver (1 Peter 1:18–19). His sacrifice on our behalf brought us eternal life. We would never want to do anything that might bring a stain upon Him or taint the good news He brought to us.

When taken to the extreme, the good desire to manifest victory will hinder us from presenting Jesus to the world accurately. To express that we have entered a state of triumphalism is a distortion of the New Testament. God promised that we are more than conquerors "in" all the troubling events of life (Romans 8:37). He did not promise we would be conquerors "over" those things. When our goal is to manifest victory, instead of experiencing Jesus, we will not be allowed the freedom to be human. This will usher in hypocrisy, and we will present to the world a false understanding of what it means to live with a good God in a bad world.

The fear, loss, hurt, sorrow, and tears of real life will be banished from our public presentation of what it means to be a follower of Jesus. Forced to play the role of the victor, we will wear a false face and Sunday smile, declaring all is well in the assembly of saints. The rest of the actors will praise our great faith. But on the inside, we are playing another role that never finds its way to center stage. We must suffer our pain—alone.

This tale of fiction must stop and be replaced with reality. We must have the courage, gained from the empowering presence of Jesus, to speak the truth. The world is hurting, and they are not afraid to say so. When these hurting ones see the fantasy of triumphalism in the church, they will not be able to relate to it.

But if we allow ourselves to be human and manifest the hurt our fellow humans are experiencing, they will be able to relate to us. And when His mighty presence empowers us to walk courageously in our manifested pain, they will be mesmerized by us. They will wonder how we are able to walk, and they will want what we have. This is when we become dangerous in the kingdom of God. They will see the power of the presence of God to help them with their pain, as He has been faithful to empower us through our pain.

Battle Fatigue

I fear that the church wants to provide the remedy of Jesus apart from the pain that requires Him as the remedy. If we disregard that kind of thinking, and dare to be honest about our struggles, we will likely encounter opposition. Some will add their voice to the chorus that we are not manifesting victory. Stand against that opposition, for you are proclaiming an honest victory to the world of hurting people.

When our daughter Avery was at the height of her struggle to survive, our mama and papa hearts were stretched to the limits. There was so much unknown with this rare disease. We had far more questions than answers, and fear loomed large in our lives. Added to the unknown was the known. Her frail little body and the puzzled faces of the doctors. We took small steps through the cardiac arrests that she valiantly fought against and overcame. Added to our fear was the battle fatigue that came from this seemingly never-ending fight. We were so weary.

A friend called to see how Avery was doing. And then she asked how Janet and I were doing. Since pain has a way of stripping off the facade we so often wear, I had decided to live in and express reality. Further, I assumed she asked because she really wanted to know how we were doing. I told her we were tired and frustrated. I shared that our hearts were crushed and we were fearful of what each coming day might hold for our family.

She did not appreciate my honesty and abruptly sought to correct what I had shared. "Well, that's not of God," she said.

"No," I told her, "But it is human, and last time I checked, that's what I am." I had so much more to say, but she had quickly become silent. I believe she realized what she had done. I did not want to abuse her, so when she apologized, I told her I forgave her. We all need to remember that when pain invades our lives, we need to allow ourselves the freedom to be human. It is right to grieve and share our sorrow.

Our Blessed Savior

When Jesus wept, He was wearing the face of faith. We, the church, must not only come to understand what this face of faith looks like, but we must also practice it. We must give ourselves the freedom to wear that face and give that freedom to others. In our human spirit, where the Holy Spirit dwells, we are at perfect rest, in peace, and security at all times. Nothing in this world can touch our spirit, which the Holy Spirit has sealed with His powerful presence (Ephesians 4:30).

Our souls, however, are another story. Our emotions can be all over the map. Our minds easily and frantically race back and forth from what we know versus what we feel. Our will is kind of stuck in the middle, with the choice to hear the voice of God or the screams of our emotions. It is all too easy to succumb to the screams. They can be so loud that it is hard to ignore them.

Consider the little question I use in my own life when pain and sorrow come knocking on my door: "I know how I feel, but what is the truth?"

This version of "But God" acknowledges my feelings and even affirms their cause. But my will chooses to not let those feelings dominate my mind. Instead, the final word I choose is the truth of what God has said. This is what Jesus did in the garden of Gethsemane. With the cross looming large before Him, He agonized in His soul. He felt the raging waves of fear at the prospect of the painful onslaught He would soon endure. He was so riddled with anxiety that His sweat was mixed with blood. Tiny blood vessels on the surface of His skin broke under the stress He felt.

This is what the face of faith looked like in our blessed Savior. Note His words. Jesus was not looking forward to what was coming. He petitioned His Father that if any other way was possible, He would take that alternate path to secure our salvation. And then He announced His formidable faith with these words: "Yet not My will, but Yours be done" (Luke 22:42). Jesus did not *feel* like going to the cross, and He did not try to alter His feelings. Instead, He acknowledged those feelings. He embraced them as right and proper for anyone in agony. But then He exercised His will and *chose* to live in accordance with the revealed truth and will of His Father. This is the true face of faith.

Jesus honestly manifested on the outside the grief and sorrow that were taking place on the inside. Like Him, we do so while choosing to trust that God will accomplish His good work in our lives. With fear on our faces and confidence in our hearts, we walk into this world with the expectation that God is with us and will provide Himself to us. As He journeys with us, we will be more than conquerors in all that comes against us. We will agonize, but we will do so triumphantly because we know it is a good agony. The darkness will be an opportunity to magnify the light and love of God that is not only sustaining us but also empowering us to walk through that darkness. This is the true face of faith.

Living by Faith

The prophet Habakkuk epitomizes living by faith. Heartbroken over the sinful state of his fellow Israelites, He cried out for God to intervene. God responded that He was sending the Chaldeans to discipline them for their rebellious ways. This put Habakkuk in a quandary. Yes, the Israelites were rebellious, but the Chaldeans were even more wicked. Habakkuk could not wrap his mind around how God could use a more wicked people to discipline wicked Israel. It made no sense to his brain. It was not fair.

So, Habakkuk went into his prayer room, vowing he would not come out until God gave him an answer to his dilemma. Finally, God answered. With profound simplicity, God told Habakkuk to trust Him: "The righteous one will live by his faith" (Habakkuk 2:4).

I can almost hear Habakkuk say in response, "That's it? That is all you are going to give me?"

And I can almost hear God reiterate, "Yes, Habakkuk. That's it."

Though our emotions can scream God's "answer" is insufficient, it is a reasonable call God places on our lives. The call to faith is not given in a vacuum. God has provided a proven track record of His faithful dealings with His people. His grace and goodness are confirmed throughout the biblical record. The cross stands for all of history as confirmation that the love God has for us is never to be in question.

God is absolutely holy and holy absolutely. He loves with infinite love and uncompromised goodness. He has a perfect purpose in what He is doing. Even if we do not understand that purpose, He does, and the complete goodness of His character beckons us to trust Him. This is the choice Habakkuk made, just as our Savior Jesus made when He faced His own quandary. Even though Habakkuk did not understand, he chose to believe. And then he wore the true face of faith, the same faith Jesus wore.

Habakkuk affirmed the reality of the gloom on the horizon. He was honest about what he was facing (Habakkuk 3). When the Chaldeans arrived in Israel, they would confirm the ugliness of their hearts with their wicked ways. The land would be decimated, and the people would be devastated. His words of woe are clear. The fig tree would no longer blossom and there would be no fruit on the vine. The olive yield would fail, and the fields would produce no food. The flocks of sheep would disappear, and there would be no cattle in the stalls. Life would be hard and painful. This was the coming reality for

Habakkuk's life, and he readily admitted the effect it had on his soul.

With tremendous courage and the complete absence of shame, he declared in writing:

> I trembled inside when I heard this;
> my lips quivered with fear.
> My legs gave way beneath me,
> and I shook in terror. (Habakkuk 3:16 NLT)

His uncompromising, honest declaration of faith stirs my heart. He offered no facade of triumphalism, nor did he wear a false face and a Sunday smile. He was honest. He was a man of integrity. He told of life as it really was. We must commend him for this. But he did not end his declaration there. Habakkuk also voiced his own "But God."

Pain and sorrow would not be the end of his story, because God would honor Habakkuk's faith (1 Samuel 2:30). God would meet him in his struggle and provide him with strength. God would make him like a deer, equipping Habakkuk to walk on high places. I believe those high places are the intimate experience of God that we gain as we walk through the valleys life brings our way. With eyes of faith, Habakkuk saw not only the coming devastation but also the glorious deliverance God would provide for him.

Habakkuk would affirm why the walk of faith is best described as an agony. He would embrace it as a good agony because his leap of faith will have landed him into the powerful right hand of God. Secure in God's powerful grip, Habakkuk would experience the promised presence of God. Hope would be birthed in his heart. Having chosen the agony of faith, he would stand. He would walk. He would rejoice in the God Who will be with him and provide for him, no matter what this hellish world could throw at him.

I believe with all my heart that triumphant tears fell down his cheeks as he cried out:

Yet I will triumph in the LORD,

I will rejoice in the God of my salvation.

The Lord GOD is my strength. (Habakkuk 3:18–19)

His was the true face of faith. As I ponder his journey, I think of the writer of Hebrews, who said when the people of faith are not delivered, yet continue to trust God, "The world was not worthy of them" (Hebrews 11:38 NET).

As Long as it Takes

Dear Reader, if you are seeking to get through what you can't get over, sit down in your pain. Put a stop to your denial, and your attempts to anesthetize your pain. Instead, embrace what has happened, dare to sit down in it, and cry out in faith for God to meet you there. He will sit down with you. He will wait with you as long as it takes. He will tenderly raise your head so you can look into His eyes. When you are convinced of His love and care for you, and you are ready to walk again, He will lift you up with His strong right hand. As you step back into life, still carrying the hurt, He will walk with you.

Wear the true face of faith. Let the world see your own good fight of faith. Let them see your pain, your sorrow, your loss, your grief, and your fear. But let them also see His presence in you as He walks with you through the valley of death. Feel the freedom to grieve when the pain announces its presence to your heart and soul. Choose to set your mind with your own "But God." Claim the truth of His Word that He is storing up your tears in His wineskin. Trust that He will use those tears to bring new life to you. Find Him in ways you never knew Him before. Allow Him to write a different ending to your story.

Stand in awe of His goodness as He uses your tears as the ink to document how you agonized in your own good agony. Let your story herald to the world that your present sorrow cannot be erased by the proclamation of future glory. But also herald that His *present* presence is sufficient to strengthen you in that sorrow. He may not bring deliverance from your pain. He may not answer your questions. But He will provide you with Himself, and He will prove Himself more than sufficient for you to bear up in suffering that does not go away.

As you "agonize in your own good agony of faith" (1 Timothy 6:12), claim God's incredible declaration from Hebrews 11:38 as your own. He states there that the world is not worthy of people who are not delivered from their struggle yet continue to trust Him.

Dear one, if you are journeying through what you cannot get over and continue to trust God in your journey, hear what the Spirit says to you:

The world is not worthy of you.

The world is not worthy of you!

CHAPTER 17

When the Pain Feels Too Great: Suicide

Her terrified voice shrieked through my phone as I said hello. Instantly my mind raced, and my heart felt like it stopped. I braced myself as I have had to do many times over the years. This was not going to be a normal phone call. Her horrific screams distorted her words, making it hard to understand what she was saying. When I asked for clarification, she made a huge effort to speak clearly, but with an ever-greater volume and intensity in her voice. She desperately wanted me to understand the horror that had invaded her life. "He's going to kill himself!"

My job as a pastor is to communicate, but I can't describe the effect those words have on a human being. They numb the mind and overload the thought processes with the horrifying reality of what is happening. Yet strangely, those words bring an overwhelming sense of non-reality as well. Questions pour into the brain faster than they can be processed. *What? How?* And of course, the ever-present, unanswerable, and disparaging question, *Why?*

Before I could open my mouth to respond, horrible memories flooded my mind. Not long before, I had received a similar phone call from my sister. She spoke with the same terrified voice. She had the same horrific screams that distorted her words. And when I asked her to speak clearly so I could understand, I heard the words that I now cannot stop hearing. My nephew Josh had taken his life.

I immediately shut down the memories of my nephew flooding my mind, or the raging emotions would have left me paralyzed. That is what the suicide of a loved one does to you. It knocks you to the ground. Though your mind races, your chest heaves, and your voice screams, the rest of your body shuts down in horror. That awful choice was about to be made again. Another wounded heart was ready to put an end to their life. I needed to be fully attentive to the situation at hand.

I asked the terrified woman if her husband was willing to talk to me. He agreed, and she said they would be at my office in ten minutes. I prayed. I waited. And I wondered how the Holy Spirit would lead me in this desperate battle between life and death.

She called and said they were outside, but he would not come in. If I wanted to talk to him, it would have to be on his terms. Not a good sign. A manifestation of control is usually a sign that the person has made their decision, and they will not be easily moved away from it.

The Standoff

I continued to pray as I went outside. This strong, hard-working, confident man that I have known over the years was a shell of the man I saw. He looked disheveled and so very tired. He did not have the desperate look I've seen in my office so many times. The determination on his face, despite his weariness, was another indication that his threat was real.

When I asked what was going on, he would not look at me. His eyes were buried in his hands, but he was firm and direct with his words. "I'm going to kill myself," he said.

"Do you have a plan?" I responded.

Instantly he affirmed that he did—and even provided the details.

This was serious. Life was hanging in the balance. Continuing to pray that the Holy Spirit would guide me, I put my hand on his shoulder and announced as gently and compassionately as I could, "You don't want to kill yourself."

He took his hands away from his eyes and lifted his head. With what seemed to be a hint of disgust, he told me that yes, he did want to kill himself and was going to do so.

I stood my ground and gently but firmly repeated to him that he did not want to kill himself.

"Who are you to tell me what I want," he grumbled.

We were in a standoff. And then these stunning words poured out of my mouth. "You don't want to kill yourself. You just don't want to hurt anymore."

No words came forth from his lips, but his eyes spoke volumes. The truth had been brought to the forefront of his mind. The lie he had been believing was exposed and lost its power. The floodgate that was holding back his tears crumbled at the revelation of truth, and he wept.

Through his tears, he affirmed to me, "Pastor Frank, you're right. I don't want to kill myself. I just don't want to hurt anymore. I want the pain to stop."

I placed my hand on his shoulder, affirming him as the tears flowed freely now. The initial heaving sobs that took control of him were now giving way to a gentler, sustained release of the sorrow that he had been holding inside.

A State of Desperation

As I pondered what was happening with him, an illustration I have used with others came to mind. When the sorrows of life haunt us monotonously and assault us perpetually, we face every day like a pressure cooker. The constant barrage of grief heats up the turmoil of trauma in our soul, turning our inner being into a bubbling cauldron. As the pressure inside continues to build, we grow desperate. We search for some way, any way, to alleviate the devastation. But unlike a pressure cooker, no button can release the pent-up sorrow and despair those wounds produce. We are one breath away from our desperation turning into obsession. We must end this pain. That thought dominates the mind so powerfully that other thoughts are not heard. It is like being in a tunnel that takes us deeper into the darkness, where no light is able to break through.

In our frantic search for relief, we may begin to contemplate that ending our life is the only way out of this desperate state. We call it suicide, defined as the intentional act of taking one's own life. Though that is correct, I find it cold and sterile. That word deals only with the act, the choice to end a life. This inadequate definition fails to consider *why* someone would take their life. Suicide is a word that offers no attempt to understand their decision or extend compassion. It's just suicide. It happens. It's sad.

I have begun using a different term, one that better defines the level of desperation occurring in the soul of someone who would make such a drastic decision. I prefer to call it *painicide*. Most people do not really want to end their life. Like the dear man in the story, they just don't want to hurt anymore. Their pain has become so painful they will do anything to stop it.

Illegitimate Means

Dear reader, I need you to know that I am not writing these words from my study. I am writing them from the lab of personal experience. At a point in my life, the pain was so ominous that not even the love of family and friends was powerful enough to deter the obsessive pursuit of freedom from the pain. It did not matter what it took to accomplish that desperately sought-after goal. I had to stop the hurt.

I had the thought.

I had the plan.

Before I could act on that plan, my eyes were opened to a glorious truth from God's Word. A light did break through my tunnel of darkness. If you have these thoughts and a plan to end your hurt through *painicide,* please do not act upon them. Please continue reading. *Painicide* is an illegitimate means to end your pain. There is another way.

Illegitimate? This word likely makes you angry, but I believe it to be correct. I offer it to you with a purpose. My goal is to make you think clearly and fully before you make such a dramatic, devastating, and permanent decision. That decision would not only affect you but also the ones you love and who love you.

Ponder the meaning of that word. *Merriam-Webster* defines it as "not rightly deduced or inferred; departing from the regular; not sanctioned by law." This powerful word screams against its own existence as something we should not elect to pursue. It is a word of contrast. The existence of something illegitimate means there is also a path or choice that is legitimate. A *legitimate* path is right, reasonable, authentic, and warranted. Consider these last two words.

Authentic means something is real and dependable, and that is why it is warranted. It is a choice worth making. It is a choice we need to make. When we are contemplating taking our own life, we must ponder the decision and deal with its unsoundness compared to the existence of a credible choice to not take our life. You have already pondered the illegitimate path. But you need to consider the legitimate one.

The Enemy's Destructive Agenda

The message of *painicide* is, if I die I will be free. It offers a way out of the pain, but it comes with paramount devastation in the lives of those left behind. This path to freedom is destructive. This choice puts you in harmony with the destructive goal of the Enemy. Jesus told us that Satan seeks to steal, kill, and destroy (John 10:10). When you choose to take your life, you join the ranks of those who bring havoc to humanity.

We must recognize this destructive agenda the Enemy offers, but it will not be easy. The waves of desperation that pound our minds make it hard to hear the voice of others, especially our Comforter, the Holy Spirit. But we must hear His words. Jesus said we can hear His voice (John 10:27), even when the Enemy is screaming loudly or whispering in our ears like an illicit lover. The Holy Spirit warned us in 2 Corinthians 11:14 that Satan comes to us masquerading as an angel of light. His word choice is revealing. *Masquerade* means to deceive, pretend, or cover something up. Satan cannot be trusted, and we must be on guard that what he offers is gravely suspect. He comes with ulterior motives. What he brings may appear bright and gleaming, but it is dark and grievous.

Our Enemy is dangerous. He is known as "the father of lies" (John 8:44). His weapon is the lie. But when he comes as an angel of light, he offers us so much truth that it is hard to recognize the lie hidden in his offering. That lie, once believed, will unleash in full force the destruction he intended it to bring, and devastation will reign. Do you want to ally with the destroyer? Is it your true heart to participate in his wicked agenda? Stop. Think. Reason.

The path to freedom Satan is offering you is illegitimate. His radically twisted path will end your life tragically, and you will extend pain to your friends and family. You may end your agony, but you will give them a massive dose of grief, the very thing you are seeking to escape. If you make that choice to kill yourself, you will have joined the Evil One's ranks as a destroyer. Though offering freedom from your hurt, *painicide* is a destructive path.

The Legitimate Path

I chose another way. The path of truth is constructive instead of destructive, authentic and warranted. Many others, who have walked into my office with their own pain and a plan, have chosen the same path, including the dear man mentioned above. Together, we no longer have a plan to end our lives but a purpose to fulfill it. This legitimate path will not end the hurt, but it will provide a way through it. God has promised this to those who trust Him. It is not an easy path to follow. It can be tortuous, but this journey has a true and powerful destination.

In seeking Him, we will find Him, not the knowledge *about* Him, but the experience *of* Him. He will be all He is to us, and He is God. He will be our strength when ours has been depleted. He will be our courage when we are paralyzed with fear. He will be our peace amid our anxiety. He will be our hope when we are hopeless. That is His promise (Jeremiah 29:13).

When the nation of Israel found themselves in a hopeless state, their prophets began to prophesy that God had abandoned them and chosen another people. This was a slander against the character and faithfulness of God. In response, God did a little prophesying of His own. He disavowed those prophets and their prophecies. We all need to hear His words: "'Do not let your prophets who are in your midst or your diviners deceive you, and do not listen to their interpretations of your dreams which you dream. For they prophesy falsely to you in My name; I have not sent them,' declares the LORD" (Jeremiah 29:8–9).

When we are in the desperate state of contemplating taking our own lives, we are unable to filter through the voices. Did you grasp what God said about these voices? Do not listen to them. He did not send them. We need to *screen* our thoughts and reject any thought that does not line up with the voice of God. Listen to what He *did say* to the hurting people of Israel as they experienced failure, rejection, emptiness, and hurt:

"I'll show up and take care of you as I promised. I know what I'm doing. I have it all planned out—plans to take care of you, not abandon you, plans to give you the future you hope for. When you call on me, when you come and pray to me, I'll listen. When you come looking for me, you'll find Me. I'll make sure you won't be disappointed...I'll turn things around for you. You can count on it." (Jeremiah 29:10–14 MSG)

This is God's promise to you too. His glorious, compassionate, hopeful words are for anyone who is hurting and struggling to take even one more step in a world that is robbing them of the joy of living: "Call on Me. You won't be disappointed. I'll turn things around for you."

Please do not choose the illegitimate path of *painicide*. Please choose the legitimate path of taking God at His Word and letting Him prove His goodness and faithfulness to you. Cry out to Him. Call on His name, Jesus, and find Him as the psalmist did:

The Lord is near to the brokenhearted
And saves those who are crushed in spirit (Psalm 34:18).

He will save your life, make it worth living, and you will dance again.

WHEN THE PAIN FEELS TOO GREAT

.